It's Our Children's Default, Stupid

By

James L. Butler
M.S. International & Corporate Finance
Walsh College of Business Administration and Accountancy

Edited by

Christopher C. Wahlberg

raptorravine@comcast.net

https://www.facebook.com/raptorravine

http://www.linkedin.com/in/jameslbutler

ISBN-13:978-1497504288
ISBN-10:1497504287

https://www.facebook.com/raptorravine

Printed in the U.S.A

First paperback printing June 2014

Book and cover design by
James L. Butler

Dedication

To: Henry Ford, Ralph M Hawtry,
and The Earl of Caithness

"It is well enough that people of the nation do not understand our banking and money system, for if they did, I believe there would be a revolution before tomorrow morning." Henry Ford, founder of the Ford Motor Company.

"Banks lend by creating credit. They create the means of payment out of nothing. " Ralph M Hawtry, former Secretary to the Treasury.

"… our whole monetary system is dishonest, as it is debt-based… We did not vote for it. It grew upon us gradually but markedly since 1971 when the commodity-based system was abandoned." The Earl of Caithness, in a speech to the House of Lords, 1997.

四 - Butler

六 - Butler

The Reading of the Last Will & Testament of:

Boomer B. Gone
January 1, 1947 – March 26, 2014

To my wife:
I leave our mortgage with a balance of 122% of fair market value of the house.

To my son:
I leave two cars worth $5,000 less than the 84 month loan balances on them.

To my daughter:
I leave my phone number so debt collectors for the $12,714 in outstanding balances on the credit cards I let you borrow can reach you.

To my unemployed grandson:
I leave your $62,413 student loan I co-signed with you now in default.

To my dog:
I leave what is left of your fifty pound bag of dog food I have been living on for the last year.

Is "The Default Generation" Nearly Upon Us?

We hear it almost every day;

"We are burdening our children with a huge debt."

No, we are not. When the time comes for our children to pay the debts we left for them, they are going to say;

"Forget you! I'm not paying your debts!"

What we are burdening them with is a huge default on our debt. And when they refuse to pay our debts, the economy will fall as it has been running on debt expansion for the last 50 years.

As I have studied the history of debt growth in the U.S. economy, it has become apparent that we have reached a historic point. At no time in human history have so many people been able to borrow so much money so quickly with so little accountability. In fifty short years debt has gone from being a luxury for a few to a convenience for many to an addiction for most to a disease for all. It is a virus that has spread to every aspect of our economy from a consumer using a credit card to buy a $0.75 candy bar in a vending machine to a government borrowing $17 trillion to keep the lights on. It is this fact that we are in uncharted waters that makes it pretty much impossible for anyone, including Nobel Prize winning economists to know what will happen next.

The federal debt has been well publicized and heatedly debated, but it may not be the U.S. federal debt that is the most serious threat to the economy. A growing number of economists believe it is our huge total debt which includes our much larger private debt that is the most dangerous.

The Economist reported on a new study of the relationship between private debt growth and recessions by Alan Taylor in its September 4, 2012 edition. The study looked at debt growth and recessions in 14 major economies between 1870 and 2008. Mr. Taylor found that rapid growth in private debt was a better predictor of recessions than increases in public debt, growth in money supply or trade imbalances. (The Economist)

Despite this study, there is still great resistance by most current economists to factor in or consider private debt growth in their economic models.

The Concept of a Debt Based Economy

Think of the United States economy as a large balloon. The surface is our economic activity, or Gross Domestic Product. The air filling the balloon causing the surface to expand is our debt. The more air that is added, the more pressure there is on the surface, increasing the strain on our economy. Increasing the temperature of the air in the balloon increases the pressure even more, and rising interest rates are the flames that turn our debt into a raging inferno.

At first, the surface of the balloon expands easily with a small amount of air and little pressure. But as the balloon gets bigger, it takes an increasingly larger volume of air to get the same amount of surface expansion while building pressure on the surface, risking a rupture.

If a rupture occurs, the air escapes and the surface contracts rapidly, resulting in a recession or worse. A sudden, large increase in defaults on mortgages in 2008 caused the balloon surface to rupture and shrink. But that was tiny compared to what will happen when our children refuse to pay our debts.

The economic theory behind debt expansion is that people borrow money to buy things like houses, cars, furniture, appliances which provide jobs to people who sell them and make them. Companies then borrow money to expand production, build new facilities, and hire more workers. All of this works together to boost the economy.

The problem is, the more debt we have, the more future income must be used to pay the debt and its interest, which reduces the money we have to spend on things. This works to slow the economy. Eventually the negative effect of the debt load becomes stronger than the positive effect of the added spending and a recession is triggered, or worse.

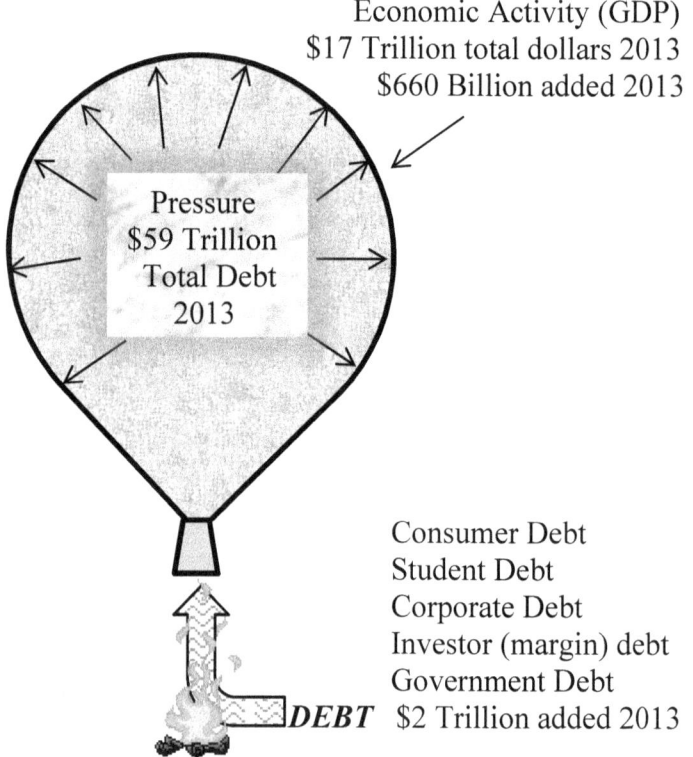

Economic Activity (GDP)
$17 Trillion total dollars 2013
$660 Billion added 2013

Pressure
$59 Trillion
Total Debt
2013

Consumer Debt
Student Debt
Corporate Debt
Investor (margin) debt
Government Debt
DEBT $2 Trillion added 2013

Interest Rates
On the rise in 2013 and going forward

Figure 1

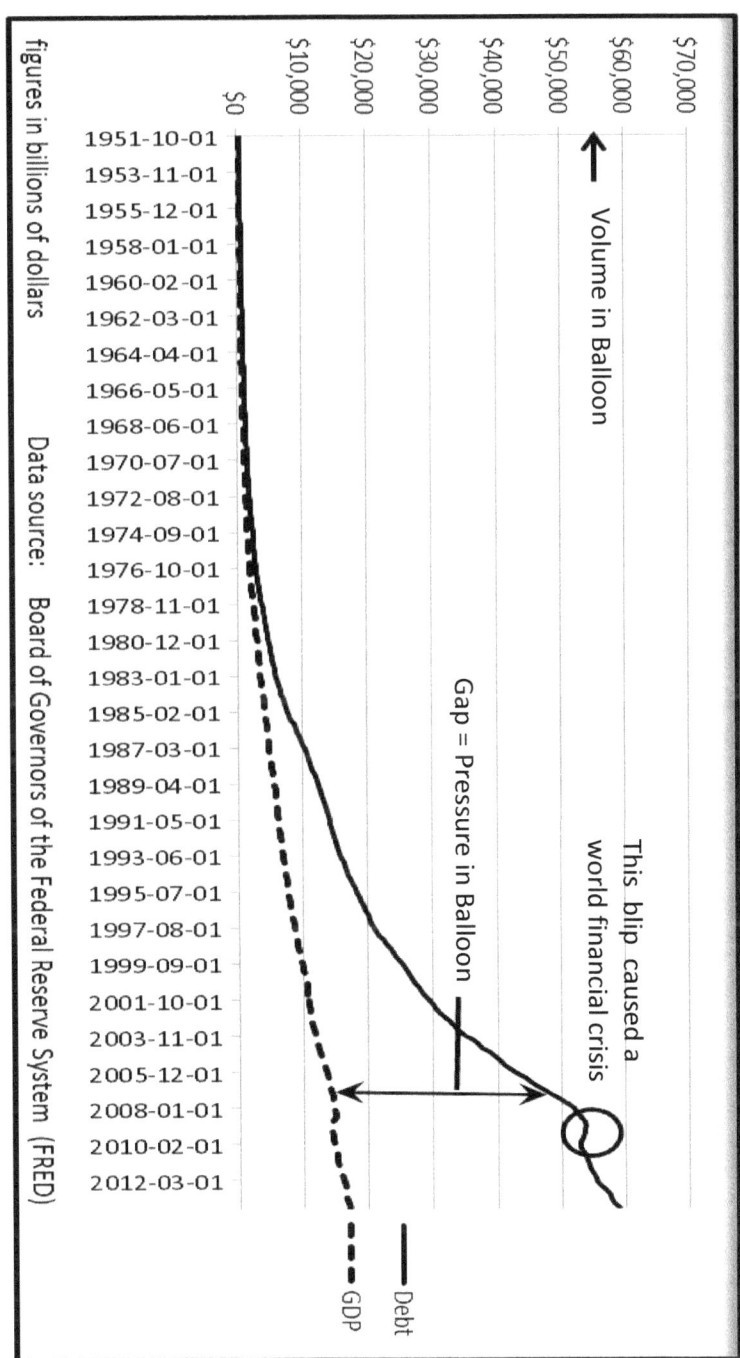

graph 1

The Real Numbers

The Federal Reserve Bank of St. Louis released the current data for the total debt in the United States Economy on March 9, 2014; All Sectors; Credit Market Instruments; Liability, Level (TCMDO).

Data from the Federal Reserve Bank of St. Louis
(Figures in In billions of dollars)

Quarter	Debt	GDP	Gap
2013-01-01	$57,406	$16,535	$40,871
2013-04-01	$57,605	$16,661	$40,944
2013-07-01	$58,039	$16,912	$41,126
2013-10-01	$58,914	$17,089	$41,825

Total Debt
2012:Q4 – 2013:Q4 increase of $2,009 billion

GDP
2012:Q4 – 2013:Q4 increase of $ 660 billion
Table 1

Debt by the Decade

A major change in the monetary policy, financial management and budget priorities of the United States occurred in the 1960s that has been carried on through the next 5 decades by every administration regardless of political party affiliation. It was not an accident. The people in charge of the money knew what they were doing and what it would become in the future, but the future was well beyond their political careers. They were content to reap the short-term benefits without concern for the long-term consequences.

The Care and Feeding of Frankenstein Debt

Debt 1950 – 1959
Total Debt 1950 - 1959 increase of $ 318 billion
GDP   1950 - 1959 increase of $ 223 billion

          Figure 2   Little Franky; couldn't hurt a fly.

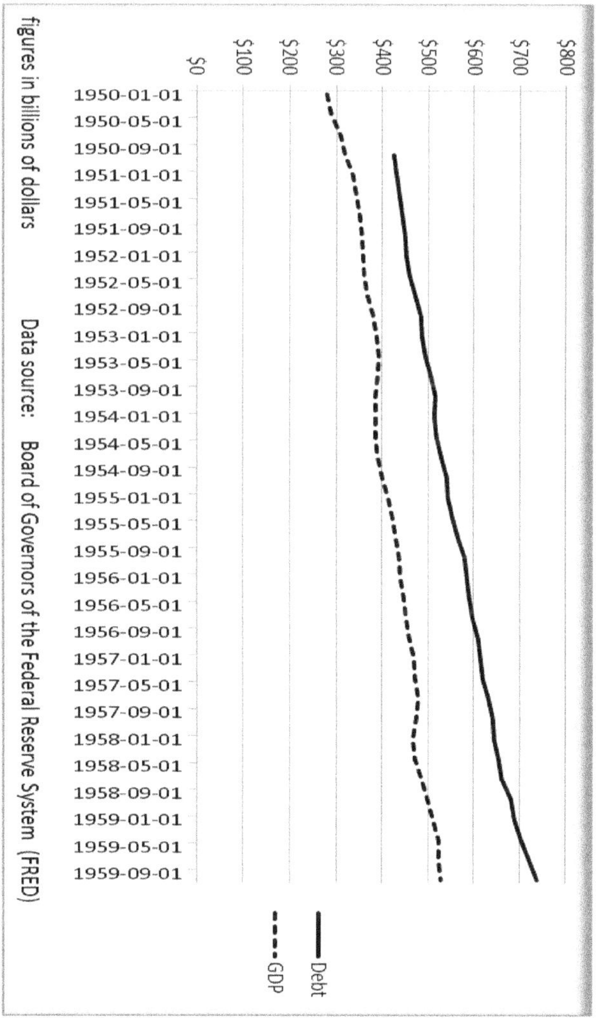

Graph 2

Debt and GDP tracked pretty much in parallel. The Korean War stimulated defense spending and government borrowing. The end of the war brought on a recession as production to support the war effort slowed down. Charge cards were coming into use with Diner's Club and American Express, but were not widely accepted and they had to be paid in full every month. A car loan was 24 months with 20% down minimum. The United States dollar was tied to gold at $35 an ounce for international trade, limiting ability for the U.S. to print excessive amounts of new paper money.

Perhaps the most significant economic event in the 1950s was one which never appeared in the financial news at the time. A great and mighty force was quietly being born in hospitals all across the nation; the Baby Boomer Generation. 76 million new consumers appeared in homes between 1946 and 1964, over 40% of the total population at the time. This generation would change the face, soul and heart of America for the next 60 years. As they flowed through each stage of their collective lives, they would leave a permanent legacy on the economy and culture of each decade they left behind.

And I am one of them, born in 1952.

Debt 1960 – 1969

Total Debt 1960 - 1969 increase of $ 727 billion
GDP   1960 - 1969 increase of $ 512 billion

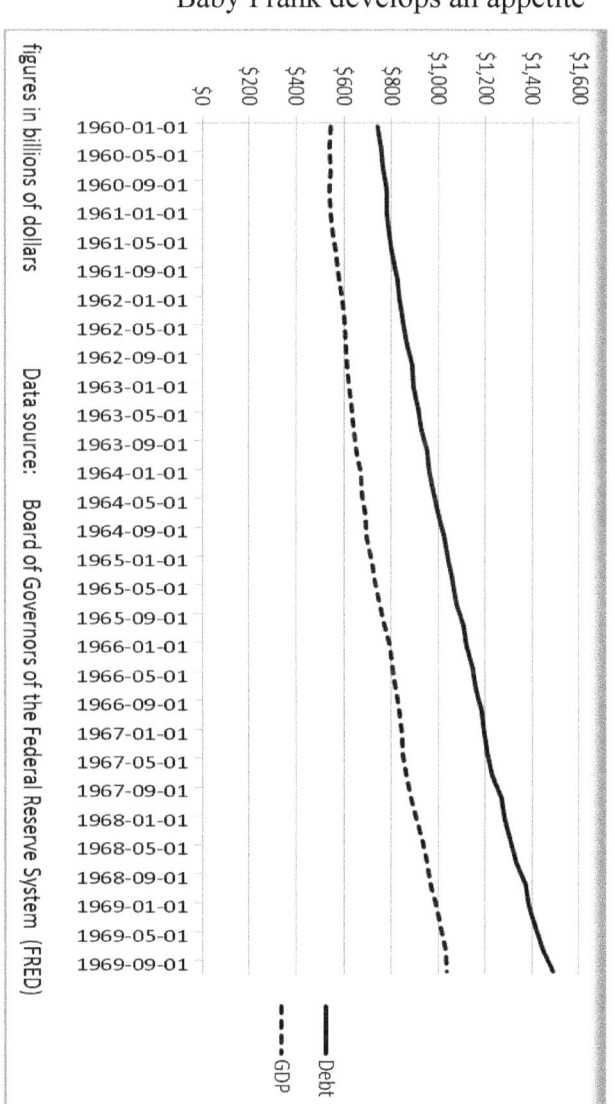

Figure 3
Baby Frank develops an appetite

Graph 3

Major changes set the path for the future of the United States economy. The Vietnam War was escalated in the mid-sixties with 500,000 troops sent in along with billions of dollars in equipment. Large new social programs were added to government expenditures at the same time; AFDC, Medicare, Medicaid, and Head Start. The US Government had to print more and borrow more to pay its bills and inflation began to ramp up.

Item	1960	1969	increase	%
New House	$12,700	$15,500	$2,800	22.0%
Income p/yr	$ 5,315	$ 8,540	$3,225	60.7%
Gas p/gallon	25 cents	35 cents	10 cents	40.0%
New car	$ 2,600	$ 3,270	$ 670	25.8%

Table 2

Bank of America launched a revolution in instant debt for instant gratification by introducing the first general purpose, revolving balance, plastic credit card with a massive marketing campaign. It became the Visa card. I still remember my parents getting their first one in 1967 and being all excited they could get a $50 cash advance to take a trip to grandpa's house for the weekend. Total debt won the race to $1 trillion and accelerated.

Demographic changes began to have an impact as well. The large bulge in population known as the Baby Boomers was moving through high-school, college and into the work force. They drove changes in what consumers bought, how they bought it and how they paid for it. Boys started buying hair spray, girls started buying jeans and hiking boots. New companies popped up overnight to serve them. Many are still around today: Nike, Gap, Land's End, Kohl's, Dominoe's Pizza, Arby's, Subway, Red Robin, Petco, and Crate & Barrel to name a few.

Debt 1970 – 1979
Total Debt 1970 - 1979 increase of $2,787 billion
GDP   1970 - 1979 increase of $1,705 billion

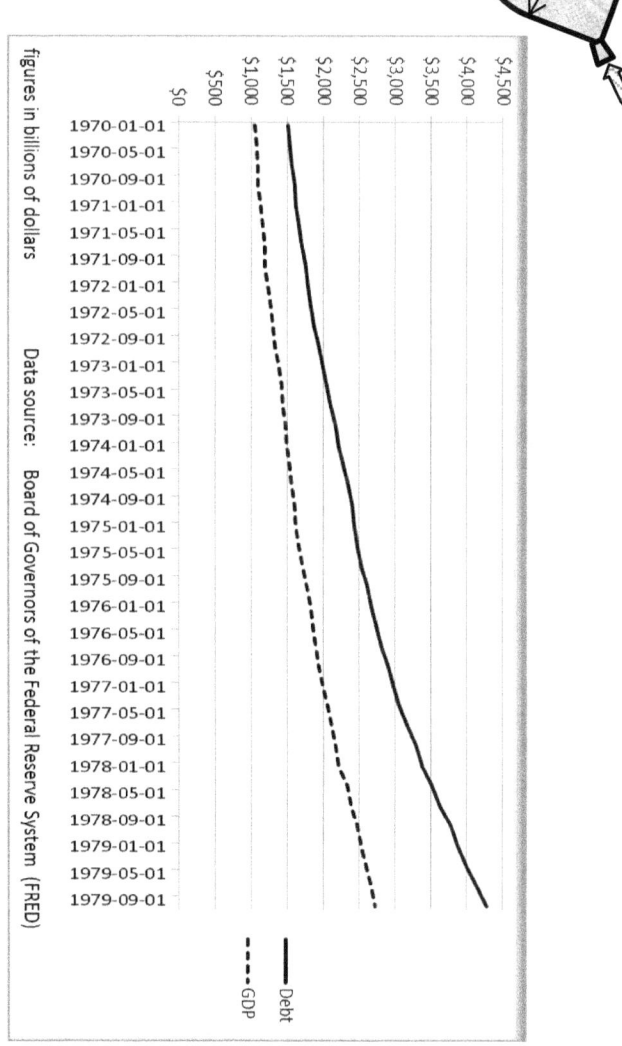

Figure 4
Frank reaches adolescence,
has issues with hormones

Graph 4

The single biggest change in how the United States manages its economy and impacts the world economy occurred on August 15, 1971. With the cost of the new entitlement programs and bills coming in for the Vietnam War, the US government could not print enough money to pay its bills with the dollar tied to gold. Countries holding large reserves of U.S. Dollars became concerned about the stability of the U.S. currency as the printing presses geared up and increased the number of dollars in circulation.

Since the U.S. dollar was still tied to gold at $35 an ounce, foreign countries began demanding gold in return for their U.S. dollar reserves. The U.S. did not have enough gold left to meet all the demands. The gold standard was officially terminated which opened the door to massive money printing, debt expansion, inflation and rising interest rates.

But why pick August 15, 1971 to do it? Many people suggested President Nixon wanted to announce it before congress was back in session. But Charles Kolb, President, French-American Foundation; and Former President, Committee for Economic Development may have given us a clue to a stronger motive to take action in a reflective comment made on November 19, 2013. According to Mr. Kolb, France joined many other nations that were demanding gold in exchange for their U.S. dollar reserves, but took a more aggressive position by steaming a French warship into New York harbor the first week of August with orders to retrieve all of France's gold from the New York Federal Reserve Bank. (Kolb)

I actually listened to and watched President Nixon's speech on television. I do not recall any mention of a French warship in New York Harbor. But I very clearly recall the President announcing a freeze on all wages and prices. He thought we could contain inflation by making it illegal. Inflation took no notice.

Economists are still debating the impact of dropping the link to gold on the world, including how it was tied to the 'Oil Shock' of the 1970s. David Hammes and Douglas Wills at the University of Washington wrote an excellent paper on how the rapid increase in oil prices and gasoline shortages for American consumers were tied to the end of the Bretton Woods Agreement called *Black Gold – The End of Bretton-Woods and the Oil Price Shocks of the 1970s.* (Hammes)

Their paper is especially relevant as the United States also became a net oil importer for the first time in its history as Baby Boomers became more mobile, started to buy cars, the number of airplanes increased and energy use climbed. The Organization of Petroleum Exporting Countries (OPEC) became an international economic power house and oil prices soared driving up the cost of everything.

The US manufacturing base got hammered by cheaper imports from Asia and other countries. Baby Boomers were much more open to buying foreign products than previous generations, especially products from Germany and Japan. They held no grudges for our enemies of WWII. Vietnam is the Boomer's personal war experience. WWII is just something they see in the movies and read about in books.

As Boomers became full-fledged consumers, credit card use expanded quickly, as did the number of auto loans while inflation climbed into double digits. Buying something today on credit that would cost more tomorrow seemed completely logical. By the end of the decade, total debt was approaching 200% of GDP.

Debt 1980 – 1989

Total Debt 1980 - 1989 increase of $ 8,418 billion
GDP   1980 - 1989 increase of $ 2,897 billion

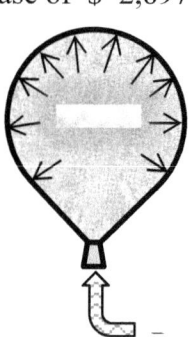

Figure 5
Frank becomes a
rebellious teenager

      The full transition to a debt based economy in the 1970s was followed closely by a full transition from a cautious savings based culture to a go for broke debt based culture in the 1980s. Anybody remember Christmas Club savings accounts? Banks offered a special 11 month savings account where people deposited a specified amount of money each month from January to November then took it out to spend on presents and the holidays in December. In January they started the process over again.

      The Baby Boomer generation wanted none of that. A dollar in the bank was a dollar to be spent as quickly as possible for them. (I am one of them.) Banks saw a great opportunity in this and built an extensive marketing campaign around it pushing 0% balance transfers, low tickler introductory interest rates, 48 month car loans at discounted interest rates and loans for just about anything else from carpet to furniture to home improvements. More importantly, they made borrowing look glamorous with commercials showing stars flashing their credit cards at fancy hotels, top restaurants and European vacations spots.

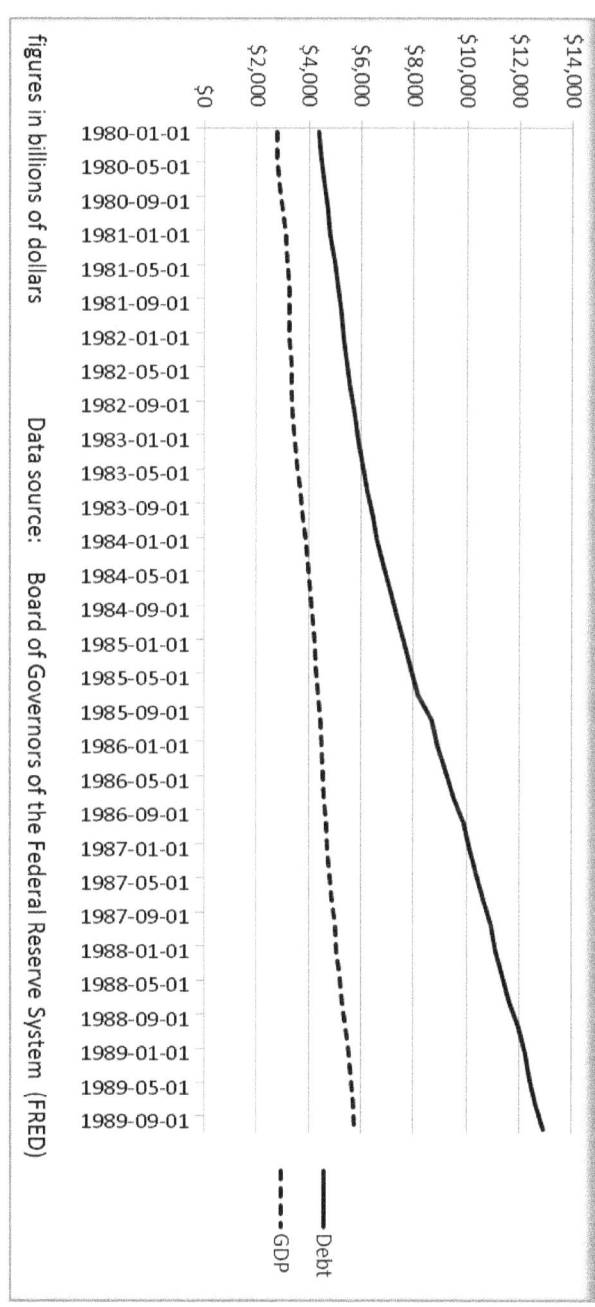

Graph 5

Sendhil Mullainathan, an economist at Harvard, studied persuasion in financial advertising. He concluded that while a single advertisement or ads from a single advertising company did little to change the overall attitude toward borrowing, the constant barrage of them from all sides made it socially acceptable to borrow more so people started borrowing more. (Story)

Consumer debt took off like a rocket. The economy powered out of recession on the burst in borrowing. The cold war was intense, defense spending was high, and China began a campaign to become the low cost manufacturer for a broad base of U.S. consumer and commercial markets. Computerized trading began to dominate Wall Street. On October 19th, 1987 the stock market fell 508.32 points, 22.6%, or $500 billion lost in one day; the largest one-day percentage drop in history. There was a brief panic but debt use did not slow down, there was no recession and debt growth accelerated rapidly into the next decade.

Debt 1990 – 1999

Total Debt   1990 - 1999 increase of $ 12,073 billion
GDP   1990 - 1999 increase of $ 4,013 billion

Frank puts on weight, drops out of high school and joins a cult to escape reality.

Figure 6

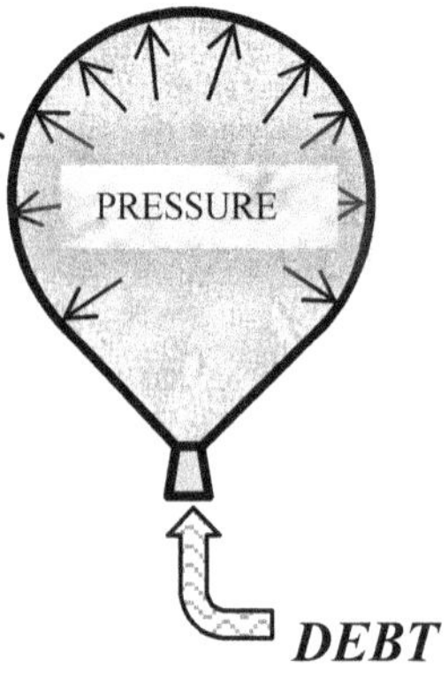

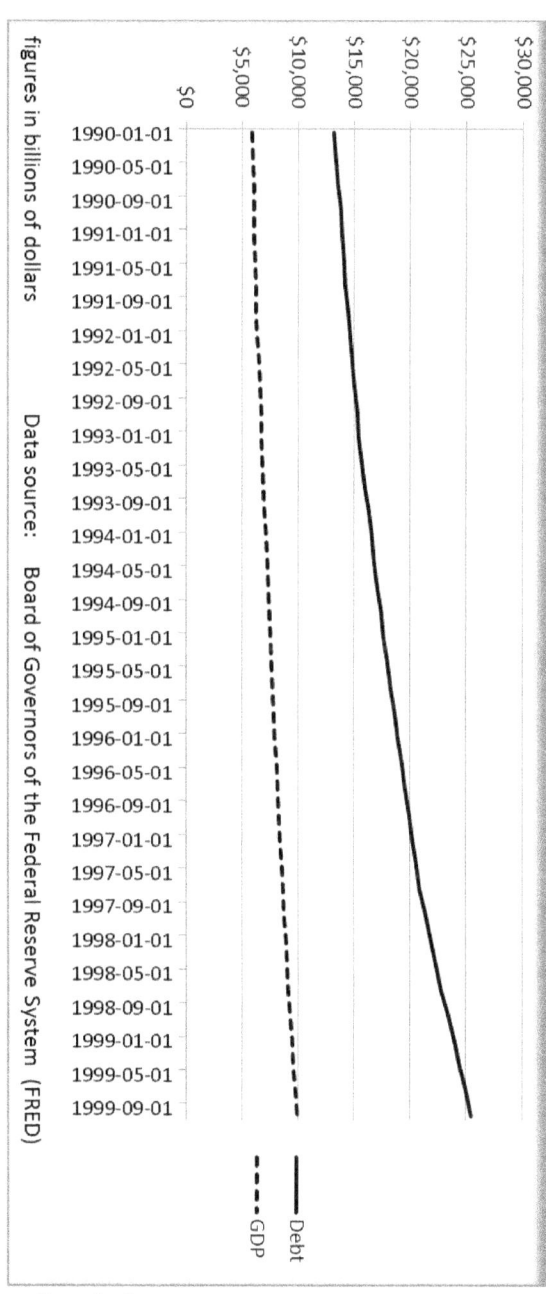

Graph 6

The early 1990s marked the end of the dominate computer mainframe era and the beginning of the internet boom. (I was working for Unisys at the time.) Virtual reality entered our vocabulary and Americans were swept up in the Dot.com craze.

Prices on big ticket items, like automobiles kept rising but the banking industry compensated by offering longer term loans, up to 60 months on a car, and new ways to buy like convertible leases. A buyer could lease a car at a lower monthly payment for two or three years then convert it to a regular 3-4 year installment loan. The problem was people went to trade in their vehicle on a new one after 4 years and found out they owed more on their loan than the vehicle was worth.

Home equity loans were pushed hard as a means to maintain or improve lifestyle as housing prices increased. Some banks would go to 125% of fair market value on a house on a loan. People took out home-equity loans to buy vehicles, take vacations or buy stocks on margin. Early investors took out profits and started a buying binge. The housing market soared riding on $12 trillion in new borrowing as the old cliché "home prices NEVER go down!" echoed across the land. Investors talked of a 'new economy' where stock prices were no longer dependent on a company's fundamental earning power. Virtual companies with no physical assets and no operating profit picked up millions of dollars in IPOs.

Then the bottom dropped out in the Dot.com crash. Asset values plummeted but all the debt remained and continued to grow at record pace, doubling in just 10 years.

Debt 2000 – 2009

Total Debt	2000 - 2009 increase of $25,771 billion
GDP	2000 - 2009 increase of $ 4,197 billion

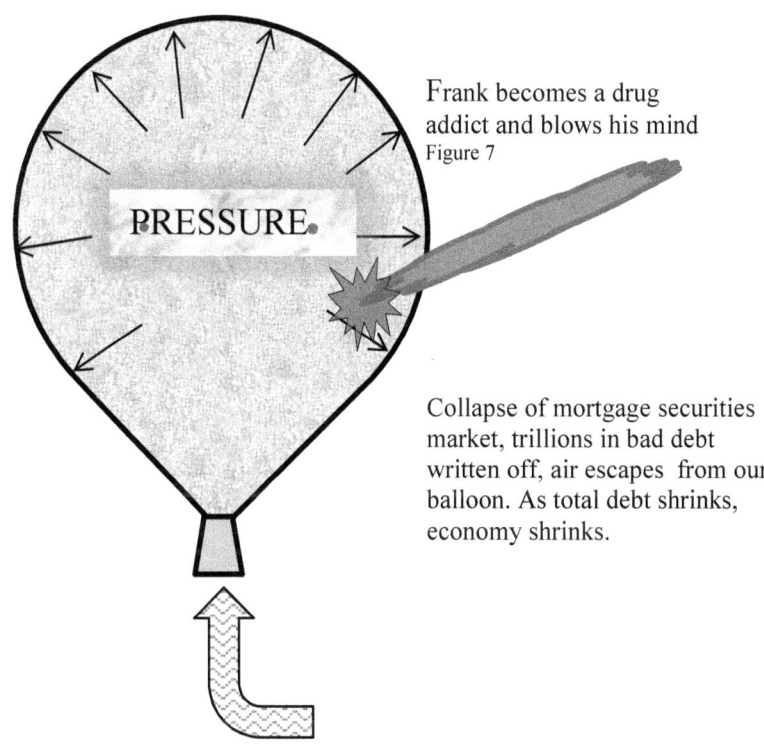

Frank becomes a drug addict and blows his mind
Figure 7

PRESSURE

Collapse of mortgage securities market, trillions in bad debt written off, air escapes from our balloon. As total debt shrinks, economy shrinks.

In response to the dot.com crash and the 9/11/2001 attack on the WTC, the Federal Reserve dumped interest rates from 7.5% to near zero which triggered explosive debt growth. Private debt was driven even harder by HUD requirements that mortgage companies make 56% of their loans to sub-prime, typically lower income borrowers, or no income in some cases. These people could not come up with the traditional 20% down payment plus closing costs, or even 10% most of the time. Many could not legitimately qualify for a loan of any kind so the

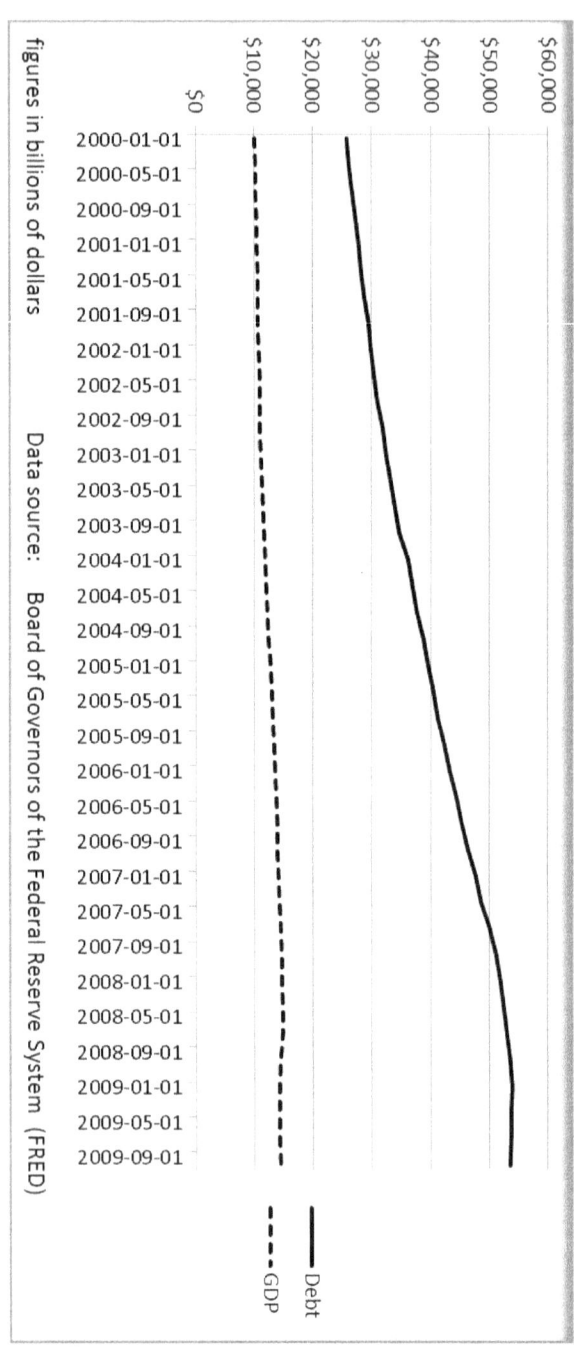

Graph 7

mortgage industry countered with $0 down, $0 cash up-front, no income verification loan packages to keep customers walking through the doors.

Consumer debt also expanded rapidly with lower rates, zero down vehicle loans stretching out to as long as 84 months, and crazy credit card use. Some studies indicated the average person had 8 credit cards and they could be used for anything anywhere at anytime.

When I worked in a major department store in 1975, a person could not use a credit card for any purchase under $20.00. In the first decade of the new century, a credit card could be used to buy a cup of coffee, pay $1.60 for an hour of parking, or by a 75 cent candy bar in a vending machine. I believe there were more places refusing to take cash than refusing to take credit cards by 2009.

As the number of students enrolling in colleges rose dramatically along with the cost of attending and the ease of getting loans to pay for it, total student loan debt began its race toward $1 trillion looking to become king of the hill in consumer debt.

More money was borrowed from 2000 to 2009 than in the previous 50 years combined. But it did not expand economic activity as expected. In the previous decade, $12 trillion in added debt generated $ 4 trillion in added GDP; or you could say added debt was 300% of added GDP. In the first decade of the new century it took over $25 trillion in added debt to get the same $ 4 trillion in added GDP; aka added debt was over 600% of added GDP.

In simple terms, the burden to pay back the debt plus interest grew much faster than the ability to pay back the debt plus interest. The mortgage market was the most critical problem, but all sectors struggled and bad debts were written off in all of them as the economy slowed dramatically and the Great Recession began.

While the world wide impact of the financial crisis is well documented and publicized, it involved a reduction of only a tiny fraction of the total debt, a 0.2 % drop year to year from 2008 to 2009, which was all made up and surpassed by 2010.

See appendix C for all the year to year data from the FRED

Year	Total Debt in billions of dollars
2008-01-01	$53,581.83
2009-01-01	$53,489.48
2010-01-01	$53,842.79

Table 3

    Some economists are saying 2008 was just a warning shot for what lies ahead for the economy as debt keeps growing. Others say we can borrow forever, so don't worry, be happy. (Oops, that was an 80s saying.)

Debt 2010 – 2013
Total Debt 2010 - 2013 increase of $ 5,502 billion
GDP   2010 - 2013 increase of $ 2,517 billion

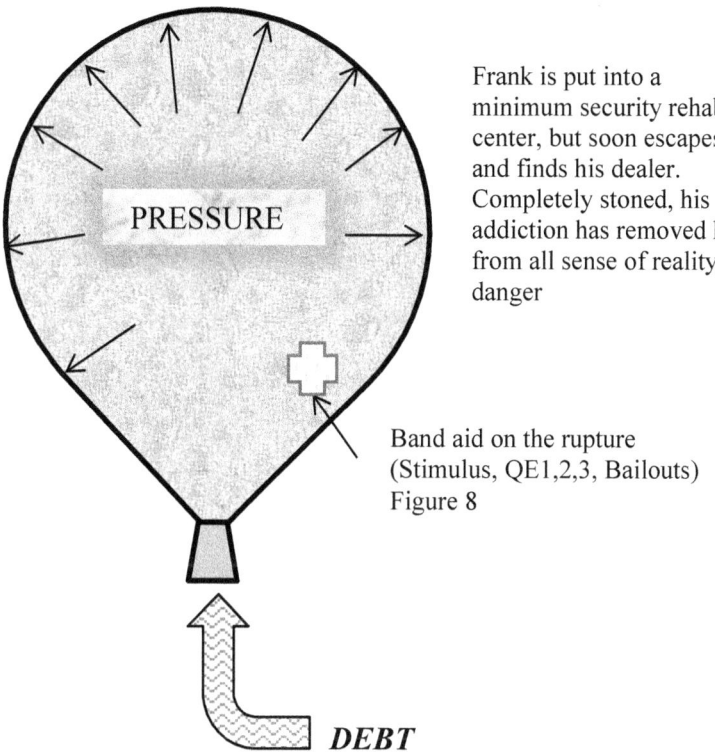

Frank is put into a minimum security rehab center, but soon escapes and finds his dealer. Completely stoned, his addiction has removed him from all sense of reality or danger

Band aid on the rupture
(Stimulus, QE1,2,3, Bailouts)
Figure 8

When private debt growth froze and deflation in asset prices struck fear in the Federal Reserve, an attempt was made to replace the private debt growth with massive growth in government debt. Band aid applied, model unchanged, debt growth expanded in all sectors. By 2010 the previous debt totals and GDP had been surpassed. Some economists said a 'Great Depression' had been avoided. But the cost was breaking all the debt records set in 2007 – 2008 by the end of 2013; consumer debt, student debt, government debt, corporate debt, margin debt, interest rates on debt increasing. It seems nothing had been learned.

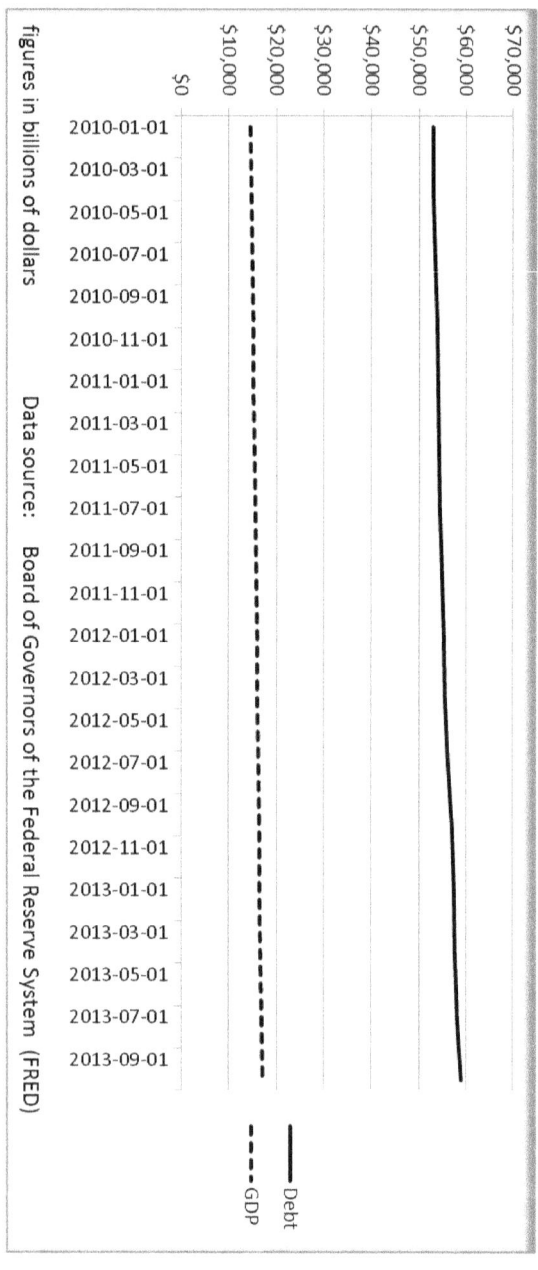

Graph 8

Summing it all Up

Tracking the growth of debt vs growth of GDP (billions)

Decade	GDP	Debt	% of GDP
50s	$223	$318	143%
60s	$512	$727	142%
70s	1,705	$2,787	163%
80s	$2,897	$8,418	291%
90s	$4,013	$12,073	301%
00s	$4,197*	$25,771*	614%
Year			
10	$667	$353	0.53%
11	$587	$1,140	194%
12	$601	$1,998	332%
13	$660	$2,009	304%

Table 4

*Note: In 2007 debt growth hit 769% of GDP growth just before total debt and GDP declined in part of 2008 and 2009, but reaching record levels by 2010.

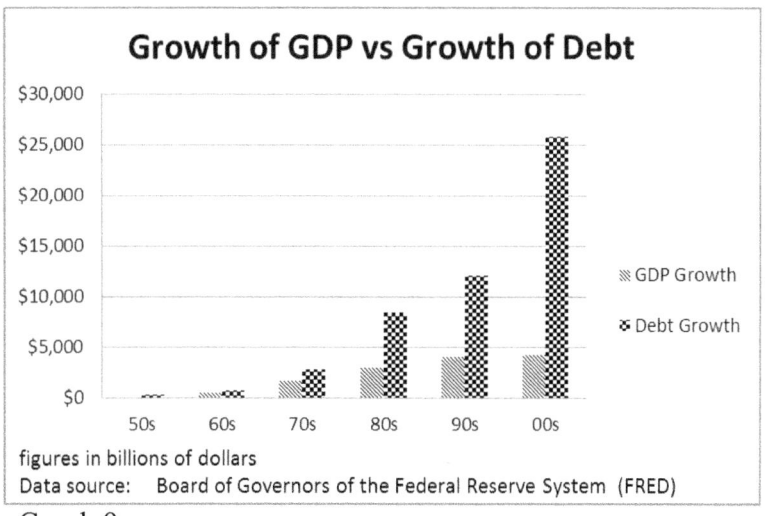

figures in billions of dollars
Data source: Board of Governors of the Federal Reserve System (FRED)

Graph 9

    This table tracking how much debt increased to produce a given level of GDP increase seems to support the principle that it takes increasing levels of debt expansion to get the same level of increase in economic activity. Notice specifically the dramatic jump in debt expansion in the 80s, the decade after the United States dropped the gold standard. And we see that doubling the amount of debt taken on in the first decade of the new century yielded exactly the same growth in GDP as the 90s.

Coming out of recession in the second decade of this century, we see debt growth over GDP has already returned to the 90s level and appears to be trending upward. Economists, even Nobel Prize winning economists continue to debate what this means to the economy as the debt load grows. I do not know how any of them could see returning to the 600% level as a good idea, but who knows.

How Government Drives Private Debt Growth

Controlling Interest Rates Banks Pay

The most influential interest rate in the U.S. economy is probably the Federal Funds Rate, which is what the Federal Reserve charges to banks to borrow from the Federal Reserve. It serves as a benchmark for interest rates charged on loans of all kinds.

The general theory is that raising interest rates slows borrowing and lowering interest rates increases borrowing. But it does not always work out that way. The private market has to have a reason to borrow no matter how low the interest rates are. If the private market does not believe it will benefit financially from borrowing money, then the debt does not expand. (Japan has been a poster child for this phenomena over the last 30 years.) Conversely, if the private market believes the money it can make by borrowing is greater than the interest it pays at any interest rate, it will continue to borrow. The 1980s proved that.

Regulating Lending and Borrowing

The federal government can also impact the growth of debt by regulation. The three best examples would be regulations on the mortgage industry concerning qualification rules, regulations on student loans concerning who can make them, and regulations on bond issuers mostly concerning who can issue bonds as a method of borrowing money.

I would also put guaranteeing loans under this category. When the government reduces or removes the risk to the lender that a borrower may not pay back some or all of the loan, the lender can be much more aggressive in making loans. This is a significant driver in the volume of student loans and mortgages issued in recent years.

Printing Money to Give to Banks to Lend

Perhaps the least understood method the government uses for influencing the growth of debt is to simply print more money and give it to the banks to loan to people; I mean buy mortgages from the banks with the intent of selling the mortgages back to investors someday, maybe, if anybody wants to buy them.

Calling this what it is 'printing money to give to the banks' is unacceptable to the financial master minds running the Federal Reserve, of course. So they made up a nice, complicated sounding financial term as a name for it; Quantitative Easing.

I think the strategy is if we have no idea what the term means, we will assume it must be a good idea.

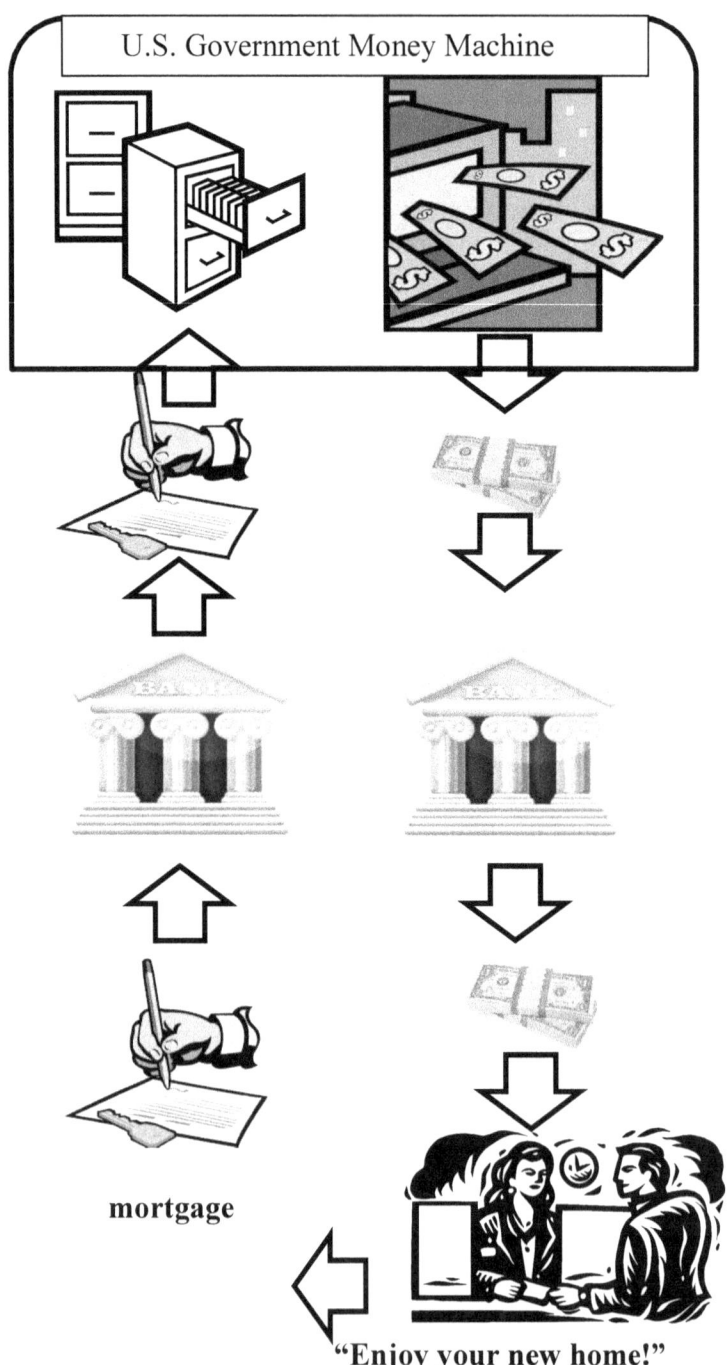

U.S. Government Money Machine

mortgage

"Enjoy your new home!"

How is the world economy doing in comparison?

Most countries are following the United States model with many growing total debt far more in relation to GDP than the United States, and paying the price for it.

World Total Debt $230 Trillion – 313% of World GDP

Meet Frank's big brother, Freddy!

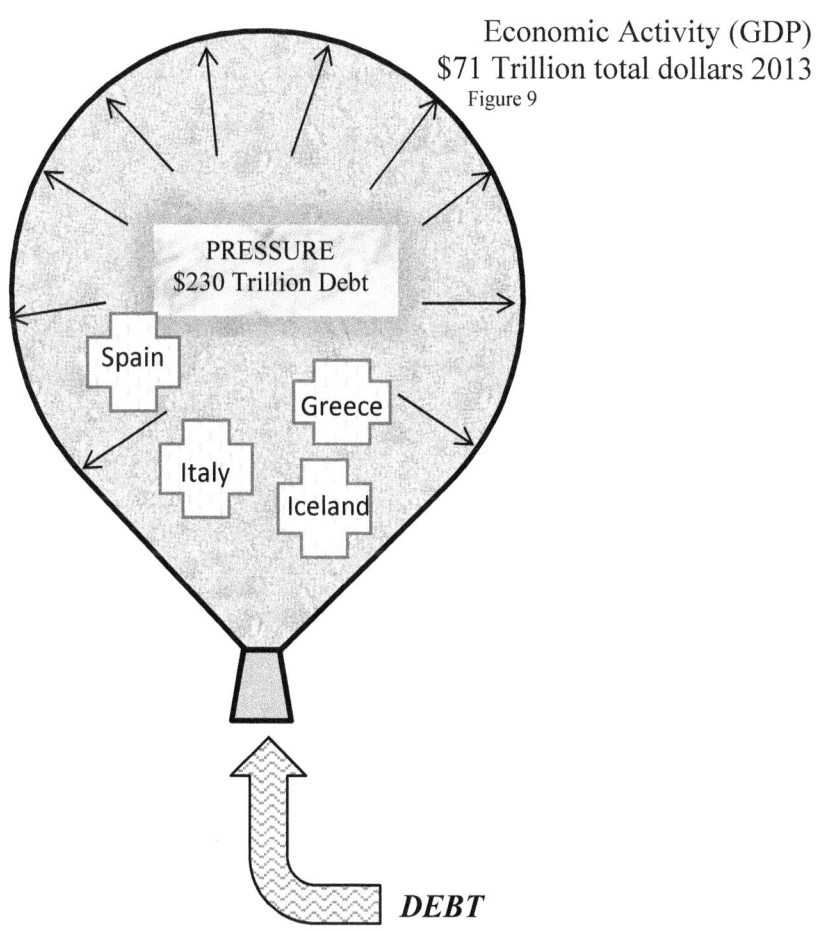

Economic Activity (GDP)
$71 Trillion total dollars 2013
Figure 9

PRESSURE
$230 Trillion Debt

Spain

Greece

Italy

Iceland

DEBT

Our Growing Addiction to Debt

A Brief History of Consumer Debt Growth

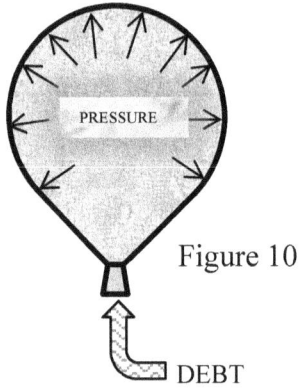

Figure 10

http://www.federalreserve.gov/
Pre-recession peak July 2008 $2.675   trillion dollars
Current debt   January 2014 $3.112   trillion dollars

The History of Credit Card Use

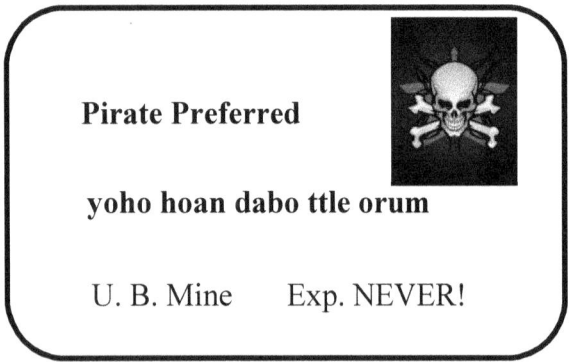

Figure 11

1900 oil companies and department stores began
     issuing their own proprietary charge cards

1946 The first bank card, named "Charge-It," was
     introduced in by John Biggins for his bank

1949 The first Diners Club Card issued

1951 The first bank credit card appeared in New
York's Franklin National Bank

1951 There were 20,000 Diners Club cardholders.

1959 American Express introduced the first card
made of plastic

1959 The option of maintaining a revolving balance
was introduced

1966 Bank of America issued the first general purpose
credit card which later becomes VISA

1966 A national credit card system was formed, the
InterBank Card Association which becomes
MasterCard

1969 Total revolving consumer debt $2.3 billion

1979 Total revolving consumer debt $47.8 billion

1989 Total revolving consumer debt $189.6 billion

1999 Total revolving consumer debt $590.3 billion

2009 Total revolving consumer debt $987.4 billion

Overall, the introduction of the revolving balance credit
card marked the beginning of a cultural revolution in terms
of attitude toward saving and borrowing. The painful
memories of the Great Depression instilled a savings
culture in America where anyone not putting at least 10%
of their paycheck into savings was being irresponsible. But
the income needed to support the huge debt burden

accumulated through the 1980s and 1990s drove the personal savings rate effectively to zero by the middle 2000s.

To make matters worse, very little of the debt was used for productive investment. It was used to live at a more luxurious level than incomes could support. While the short-term benefits of a higher standard of living seemed worth it at the time, the long term consequences proved not to be so pleasant for individuals or the economy as a whole.

The Boomers who pioneered the "borrow and spend to live better" culture are now the first to suffer from it as they have:

*Lower retirement savings

*Larger percentage of paychecks dedicated to debt service

* Increased risk of bankruptcy

* Large and unexpected expenses which create more hardship

* Increased borrowing costs on mortgages, cards, etc.

*Increased likelihood of missing payments resulting in higher fees and payments

* Become a slave to debt, reducing many options for employment, recreation, family help they would otherwise have

These downsides have not slowed the growth of the credit card industry even as the reality of the consequences hits home for many people. American consumers want a higher standard of living. The highly sophisticated advertising campaigns make them believe it is just a card swipe away. So they go for it. (Bryan)

The History of Vehicle Loans

1919 General Motors created the first automotive financing company, GMAC. Branches were opened in Detroit, New York, Chicago, San Francisco and Toronto.

1920 GMAC expanded to Great Britain.

1920 Warning issued by the Federal Reserve to all banks: "do not offer financing for automobiles used for pleasure."

1925 D.R. Crissinger, Federal Reserve "Mortagining the future earnings of the people of the United States by installment plan is a subject that merits the careful consideration of all business men and all persons who have the welfare of the country at heart" (Barnett)

1928 GMAC wrote their 4 millionth retail contract.

1970 The average length of a car loan was 3 years

2012 In the final quarter of 2012, the average term of a new car note stretched out to 65 months, the longest ever, according to Experian Information Solutions Inc. Experian said that 17% of all new car loans in the past quarter were between 73 and 84 months and there were even a few as long as 97 months.

2013 Autoloans top $750 billion

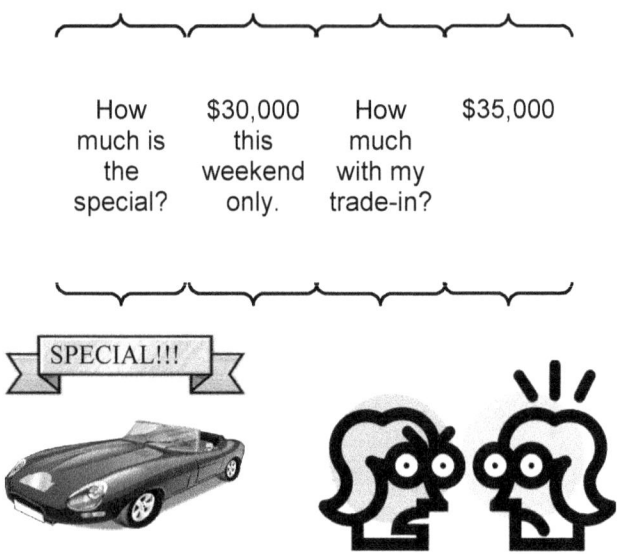

How much is the special? $30,000 this weekend only.   How much with my trade-in? $35,000

SPECIAL!!!

Figure 12

2014   *Automotive News* reports a gradual rise in trade-ins with loans underwater beginning in the third quarter of 2011 according to information from the Power Information Network.

2011 Q3	22.0% trade-ins upside down
2012 Q3	23.6% trade-ins upside down
2013 Q3	25.9% trade-ins upside down
2014 Q3	27.3% trade-ins upside down

A combination of low or no down payment required and longer loan terms of 73 to 96 months were the primary drivers. However declining prices in the used-car market also had an impact (Miquelon)

The History of Federal Student Loans

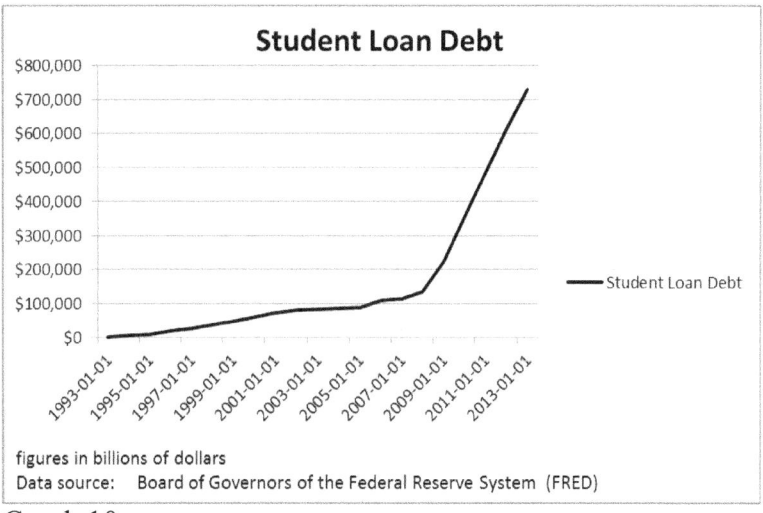

Graph 10

1958 National Defense Education Act, PL85-864
       (graduate fellowship program and the National
       Defense Student Loan Program (NDSL), the
       precursor to the Perkins Loan Program, first Federal
       student aid program for low-income students)

1965 Guaranteed Student Loan (GSL) Program,
       precursor to Stafford Loan Program

1972 Student Loan Marketing Association (Sallie Mae
       established as a Government-Sponsored Enterprise
       (GSE)

1981 Omnibus Budget Reconciliation Act (Federal
       student loans depend on financial need again   and
       add an origination fee)

1983   Student Loan Consolidation and Technical

Amendments Act of 1983 (GSL 8% interest rate, EFC)

1985 Changed the definition of a default on federal education loans from a delinquency of 120 days to 180 days.

1986 Reauthorization of the Higher Education Act Required financial need for the GSL interest subsidy, NDSL renamed Perkins Loan, created Supplemental Loan to Students (SLS) for graduate, professional and independent students, restricted PLUS loans to parent borrowers, added FFEL consolidation loans)

1987 GSL Program renamed the Stafford Loan Program

1988 Supplemental Loans to Students Reform Bill

1993 Student Loan Reform Act (established direct lending, added income contingent repayment)

1999 Direct Lending introduced loan discounts (1% reduction in origination fees and 0.25% interest rate reduction for auto debit) to compete with loan discounts offered by FFELP lenders

2002 Changed education loan interest rates from variable rates to fixed rates for new loans issued after July 1,

2006. The interest rate on Stafford Loans was set at 6.8%. The interest rate on PLUS Loans was set at 7.9%.

2005 Student loan interest rates reached historical lows. Allowed borrowers who consolidated during the in-school period to lock in a rate of 2.88%. Early repayment status loophole allowed continuing students to consolidate.

2006. The repeal was effective June 15, 2006. All borrowers could consolidate their loans with any lender. Previously, borrowers who had all their loans with a single lender were required to consolidate their loans with that lender. This increased competition for student loans, and may have lead to improved benefits and lower costs for borrowers.

2008 Congress passed the Ensuring Continued Access to Student Loans Act of 2008 (P.L. 110-227), known as ECASLA, to help avert a crisis in the FFEL program. This legislation allows the US Department of Education to buy unencumbered Stafford and PLUS loans originated from 10/1/03 to 9/30/09. The legislation also increased the annual and aggregate loan limits on the unsubsidized Stafford loan for undergraduate students and allows parents to defer repayment on the Parent PLUS loan while the student is in school and for six months afterward.

2014 U.S. student debt exceeds $1 trillion as delinquency rate increases to as high as one third.

| The feds guaranteed my student loan! | What's guaranteed about it? | That I'll never get it paid off. |

Figure 13

A History of Home Equity Line Of Credit (HELOC)

On August 15, 2008, on page A1 of the New York Times, the article titled *THE DEBT TRAP; Home Equity Frenzy Was a Bank Ad Come True* appeared, proposing at least some people in the bank industry knew they were pushing consumers over the edge.

In 1999 Citicorp hired the Fallon Worldwide advertising agency to dream up a new slogan to pitch their new home equity line of credit product offering. Fallon came up with "Live Richly". Most of the Citibank marketers loved it, but Stephen A. Cone was skeptical. He was afraid it would encourage people to live beyond their means while putting their home ownership at risk.

Citibank spent a billion dollars on the "Live Richly" campaign from 2001 to 2006 and millions of people happily responded, not to mention millions of others influenced by the ads to get HELOCS from other banks. (Story)

Other banks launched their own, similar campaigns to convince people to quit worrying about debt, or ever paying off their home, and just live well in the present because they deserved it.

There were several variations of home equity loans marketed to allow a home owner to get the largest amount in their particular situation.

1. Fixed Term Home Equity Loan
   This is basically a second mortgage where the home owner gets a specific amount of money to be paid back in a specific amount of time with equal payments every month

2. Interest Only Payments Equity Loan
   The home owner gets a specific amount of money but only has to pay the interest on the loan for a fixed term then must pay back the principle in a lump sum or finance it as a fixed term loan

3. Home Equity Line Of Credit (HELOC)
   This was the hot new product that really took off. The bank determined how much equity was in the home and issued a credit line to the customer. These credit lines would go as high as 125% of the appraised value of the home. They would also be combined with a traditional mortgage when purchasing a new home or refinancing so a home owner could end up not only paying zero down, but getting cash in hand at the closing. Of course, the down side was the home owner owed more than the house was worth the day the owner moved in.

It became more difficult to get home equity loans after the 2009 housing crisis, but not difficult enough to stop them. In 2013 $111 billion in new HELOCs were taken out according to Credit.com, (Morgan)

Are American's trying to "Live Richly" again? Maybe, or many of them could just be trying to hold their ground this time in an economy with stagnant income growth and stealth inflation.

A History of Mortgage Debt

1900   Only a few can borrow money to buy a house. Terms were usually 50% down 3-5 years payback.

1933   Federal government creates Home Owner's Loan Corporation

1934   Federal Housing Administration created

1938   Federal National Mortgage Association created, becomes Fannie Mae. Purpose is to guarantee mortgages for banks

1944   VA home loan program created

1948   Fannie Mae begins purchasing VA loans

1968   HUD and Ginnie Mae created

1968   Fannie Mae becomes shareholder owned

1970   Federal Home Loan Mortgage Corp Act creates Freddie Mac

1975   First mortgage-backed bonds created at Solomon

1981   Savings and Loans invest in ARMs

1982   Title VIII, Alternative Mortgage Transactions, Garn–St. Germain Depository Institutions Act allowed adjustable rate mortgages.

1982   Savings and Loans sell off below market mortgages in bundled securities

1986 Tax Reform Act removes all interest tax deductions except mortgage interest

1989 Freddie Mac becomes a public corporation

1992 Affordable Housing Act requires lenders meet a quota of 30% of their loans to low and moderate income borrowers, subprime borrowers

1995 Housing rules rewritten in the Community Reinvestment Act, which put added pressure on banks to lend in low-income neighborhoods

1996 Affordable Housing Act requires lenders meet a quota of 42% of their loans to low and moderate income borrowers, subprime borrowers

2000 Affordable Housing Act requires lenders meet a quota of 50% of their loans to low and moderate income borrowers, subprime borrowers

2003 Executive branch of federal government calls for increased oversight of Fannie & Freddie, putting restrictions on Liar Loans. Congress does not approve

2003 Rapid increase in low-document "Liar Loans" begins

2004 Fannie Mae reduces capital requirement for a mortgage from 10% to 5% at request of congressional minority leaders

2005 Secretary of the Treasury calls for increased restrictions on Freddie & Fannie

2005 Senate majority party introduces legislation to put restrictions on Freddie & Fannie. Minority party leader, Harry Reid, blocks it saying "we cannot pass legislation that could limit Americans from owning homes and potentially harm our economy in the process."

2006 40% of all new mortgage loans are Liar Loans

2007 Housing prices begin to fall rapidly

2008 Affordable Housing Act requires lenders meet a quota of 56% of their loans to low and moderate subprime borrowers

2008 Mortgage market collapses

2011 Federal government (taxpayers) guarantees 95% of all mortgages

2014 17% of mortgages still underwater, 9.1 million

Total mortgage debt in the United States ($millions)

1960	$190,682.000
1970	$436,392.000
1980	$1,360,402.000
1990	$3,619,826.744
2000	$6,314,594.472
2010	$14,237,745.800
2011	$13,686,625.450*
2012	$13,351,609.910*
2013	$13,148,738.850*

*The decrease in mortgage debt outstanding has not been the result of paying down mortgage debt. It has been the result of massive foreclosures and banks writing off bad debt as a result.

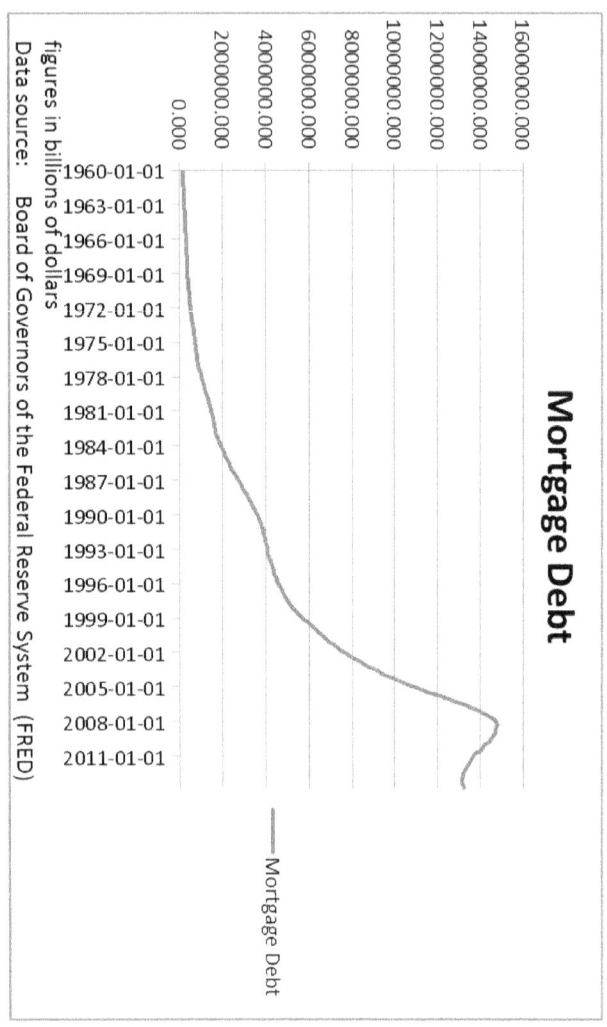

Graph 11

I have identified at least 10,000 pages of analysis, reporting, opinion, accusations, finger pointing and excuses for the 2008 financial crisis published since 2008. I have observed that they generally fall into one of six categories:

{It's her fault}

{It's his fault}

{It's their fault}

{It's certainly not my fault!}

Figure 14

1. Conservatives blaming liberal policies and actions

2. Liberals blaming conservative policies and actions

3. Liberals and/or conservatives blaming the government sponsored organizations of Freddie Mac and Fannie Mae

4. Liberals and/or conservatives blaming the commercial banking institutions

5. The banking institutions and government sponsored organizations blaming government policies

6. Independent, non-partisan, objective, outside analysts (which are very hard to come by I might add) determining that every single participant in the home loan industry from government to the person

getting the loan contributed significantly to the
2008 crisis

I find the ones in category six to be the most believable.
But even those fall short of what I have been looking for;
how the 2008 mortgage loan crisis was a part of the overall
massive growth in debt in all segments from 2000 – 2009.
They all treat the home finance industry as if it was and is
an economy all by itself, not part of a much larger problem.
Very few even tied the debt growth to the GDP growth in
that period. There were two economists who did make this
connection.

Economist Paul Krugman cautioned on proposals being
made to bring the economy back in 2009. He pointed out
that the spending that sustained the economy in the pre-
crisis years was not coming back because a large portion of
that spending came from money borrowed in the housing
boom that was not coming back. He cautioned further that a
large portion of the spending before the housing boom
came from the stock price boom. (Krugman)

Niall Ferguson went a little further and quantified the
impact of home equity borrowing on GDP growth. He
believes removing the spending that resulted from home
equity borrowing would have lowered GDP growth to a
mere 1% from 2001 to 2008. (Ferguson)

This is good, but does not go far enough in my
opinion. Almost all of this analysis ignores the fact that
every segment of debt exploded in this period: credit card
debt, car loans, government debt, student loans and margin
debt. The banks wrote off millions in bad credit card debt
almost unnoticed under the cover of the financial crisis.

So the big question I have is; what would the GDP
growth have been in 2000 – 2009 if debt growth in all
segments had been contained? Remember, the economy
saw a debt increase of $25 trillion dollars during those ten
years with only a $4 trillion increase in GDP. Mr.
Krugman's and Mr. Ferguson's analysis would seem to

confirm we are depending on debt growth to stimulate GDP growth. And the mismatch between the total debt growth and GDP would imply we would have endured 10 years of recession, or worse without the massive expansion of debt in all segments.

After studying the entire spectrum of our debt growth over the past fifty years, I have developed a slightly different take on the root cause of the 2008 financial crisis. You may or may not agree after reviewing the facts and that is fine.

I believe the 2008 financial crisis is the result of the accumulated actions of fifty years of fiscal policy striving to achieve economic expansion through debt expansion. During this period the government had strived to make it easier for more people to borrow more money in more ways faster and with less accountability than ever before. The commercial market assisted the government in meeting its objectives by not only making borrowing easier, they made it socially acceptable, even glorified it.

The bigger message in this is that nothing has changed in the basic fiscal policy of our government or the commercial marketing of debt. Just today I heard a radio ad for home equity loans telling consumers to "dare to dream" with the equity in their homes. In that lies the danger that 2008 was not the crisis, but merely the leading earthquake of a dormant volcano coming to life.

History of Corporate Debt

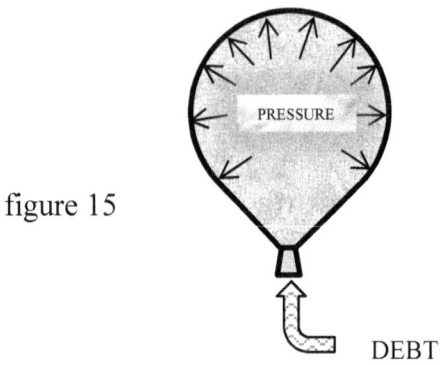

figure 15

Historically, companies have issued bonds (borrowed money) to make capital investments in their business such as building new factories, launching a new product, opening new stores or conducting new research. These are things that lead to more production, more hiring, more selling and an increase in economic activity in general. If that were the case today, record corporate borrowing might be good news. Thompson Reuters reported in the first two months of 2014, companies issued $236.6 billion in investment-grade loans, the highest on record. The last week saw $43 billion put on the market, the second-highest single-week total since at least 1980. (Cox)

However, an increasing number of companies are borrowing money to buy back their own stock. While this is does wonders for the stockholders that remain by driving up earnings per share and stock prices, it does nothing to increase economic activity.

Tech companies like IBM and Apple have lead the way in issuing bonds to get money to buy back shares of their own stock, pushing money spent on stock buybacks up 19.5% in 2013 to over $475.6 billion. While the total and annual records have been broken, the record for the largest quarter in stock buybacks is still held by the third quarter of 2007 when $233.2 billion was spent, mostly by troubled banks trying to prop up their stock prices, a strategy that failed miserably in the end. (Richter)

Corporate Debt (billions)
2013:Q4: 9,441.51
2013:Q3: 9,263.86
2013:Q2: 9,052.64
2013:Q1: 8,832.49
http://research.stlouisfed.org/

Who is buying so much of our stock?

We are.

We don't have any cash.

We borrowed it.

Who would loan us money to buy stock.

People who like that our stock price is going up.

But it is going up because we are buying it.

Not my problem.

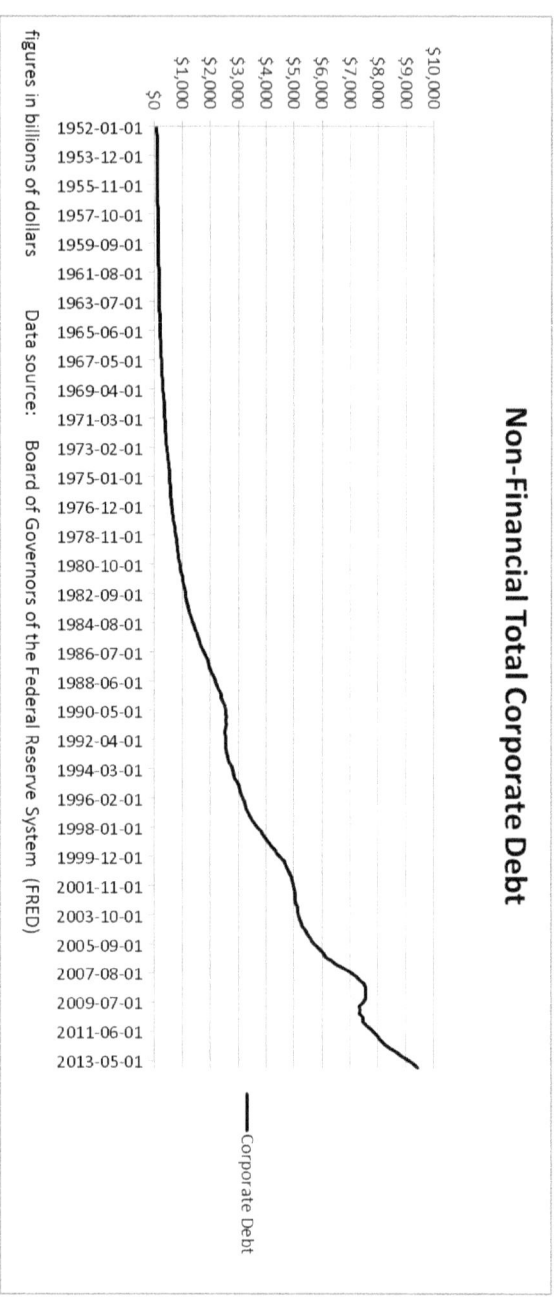

Non-Financial Total Corporate Debt

figures in billions of dollars

Data source: Board of Governors of the Federal Reserve System (FRED)

Corporate Debt

Graph 13

A Brief History of Investor Debt

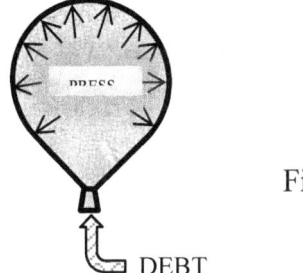

Figure 16

1920s   Investors can borrow up to 90% of their stock
        purchase from the broker

1974   Federal Reserve sets maximum margin at 50% with
        Regulation T

Total Margin Debt in Billions
1960	$ 3.3
1970	$ 4.0
1980	$ 14.5
1990	$ 28.3
2000	$198.8
2010	$276.6
2011	$267.1
2012	$330.6
2013	$444.9
2014, Feb	$465.7

When an investor has $100 to buy stocks with but
the investor wants to buy more because he is convinced the
stock can only go up, the investor borrows another $100
from his broker so he can buy $200 worth of stock. He
believes the stock will go up enough that it will pay for the
interest on the loan and bring him a profit. However, if the
stock goes down, the investor can not owe more on his loan
than 50% of what the stock is selling for on the market. He
either has to pay the broker enough cash to keep the margin

at 50% or less, or the broker has to sell enough on the investor's stock (and keep the money) to stay below the 50% mark. If the broker has to sell the stock, it drives the price lower and a downward spiral begins. So, the more margin debt there is, the greater the potential negative pressure on stock prices in a downturn.

Trim Tabs reported in March 2014 that margin debt had reached $452 billion in January and had broken the record high 7 months running. With previous rapid spikes often preceding significant declines in stock prices, many analysts are wondering if this one is a leading indicator of what is coming if not a direct cause. (Clinch)

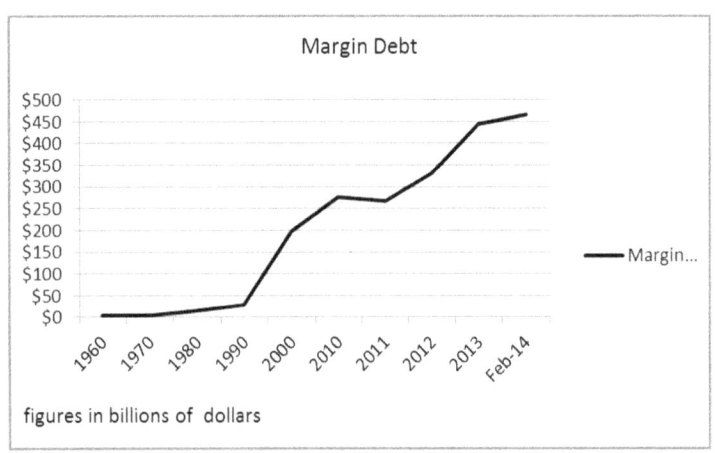

Graph 14

A Brief History of Non-Federal Public Debt

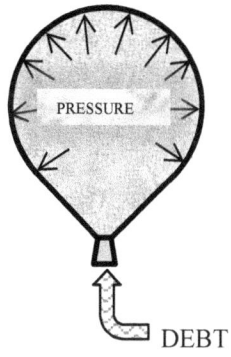

Figure 17

The status of our federal government debt has been so dramatically reported and politicized for the last 20 years there is not anything more for me to say about it. However, public debt consists of far more than federal government debt and it is in far more trouble as they cannot print money to pay the bills like the federal government can.

Since 2010 there have been 38 municipalities and 8 cities file for bankruptcy. Not all filings were granted but they still indicate the level of financial difficulty these public organizations are having in meeting bond payments along with all of their other expenses. And the pain appears to be far from over.

Stephen Moore at NewsMax thinks another 20 may face bankruptcy. Other analysts place the number as high as 40 or as low as 12, but all agree there is trouble in the public debt sector outside of the federal debt issues.

Retirement Debt; A Sleeping Elephant?

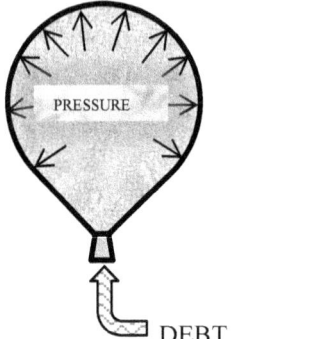

Figure 18

  The growing debt problem that could be the worst of them all has been one receiving little attention so far. It is not a specific debt segment; rather it is a specific group of people who have accumulated debt in all segments, the Baby Boomers entering retirement by the millions.

  The percent of people retiring with large debts is growing as is the amount of debt they are carrying. Instead of leaving their children and grandchildren homes with equity and savings accounts, they are leaving them with IOUs and moving in with them after losing their home.

  The Consumer Financial Protection Bureau estimates that 30 percent of all homeowners 70 and older have mortgages to pay off which has risen from 8 percent in 2001 according to the Federal Reserve's Survey of Consumer Finances, published in 2010. (Prevost)

  Large numbers of retirees facing disabling debt is far more troublesome than any other age group. When someone with decades of work life ahead of them gets into financial trouble, there is always some chance they will recover enough to settle the debts they have accumulated then build a more financially secure future. At a minimum, they have the chance to become solid taxpayers and indirectly put some of the financial assistance they may have received back into the system.

When retirees reach a point where they are unable to pay their debts, it is game over. Either the lender will have to write the debt off, which is an expense covered by others borrowing, or the children will get stuck paying the debt, or the taxpayers will end up footing the bill as they did in the 2008 mortgage crisis. The impact is already being felt.

Pretty much every survey and study being conducted indicates the Boomers are unprepared to end their working days. Some agencies report as many as a third of the bankruptcies they handle are for clients over 50. And the AARP has found that 34% of older Americans are still borrowing on their credit cards just to pay for living expenses like groceries, utilities and mortgage payments. As they hit the limit on their credit cards, they must endure the constant harassment of debt collectors which 50% of older Americans already are. (Brooks)

| Ok, a bag of Lick-um dog food and some noodles. | Yes. Put it on my credit card, please. | Lots of seniors buy Lick-um. Dogs must love it. | Wouldn't know. Don't have a dog. But it makes its own thick gravy. |

An Economist's Most Feared Word: Deflation

While deflation is technically defined as a lowering of prices and asset values (the opposite of inflation), it is important to remember asset prices in the United States are largely supported by the ability and willingness of buyers to borrow and spend. Thus, when our debt machine slows down, causing our balloon to lose air and deflate, asset prices drop as well. Remember what housing prices did in 2009? And stock prices?

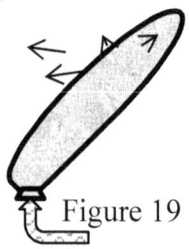

Figure 19

   Deflation can impact every sector of the economy, some more than others. Debt is one of the more severe areas.
   One line of thinking people use to rationalize borrowing money is that what they are buying today will be more expensive tomorrow, or next month or next year. That goes out the window when it is obvious what they are buying will be less expensive in the future. So they do not borrow money to buy it. In fact, they delay buying it until they can buy it for less money.
   Deflation also presents a much bigger problem to the economic policy managers in the government. When inflation is high, the policy managers can raise the interest rates as high as needed to put the brakes on borrowing and slow the economy down. But when people decide they do not want to borrow and spend anymore, the most the policy managers can do is lower interest rates to zero. But even at zero, it makes no sense to borrow money when things are going down in price, especially for larger purchases where a borrower almost instantly owes more than the item they purchased is worth. (Michael)

A National Debt Strike Looming?

What if everyone refused to make their debt payments for a month? I am seeing this question pop-up here and there in chats and comments, mostly from student organizations and people involved in the Occupy Movement. Just the threat of it would frighten the finance industry to death and possibly force some concessions. It would be an economic disaster, but could be what our children see as their only way out of the mess we are leaving for them. One failed attempt to turn the chat into action occurred in Zuccotti Park while it was filled with Occupy Wall Street protesters in the fall of 2011.

Andrew Ross, a middle-aged NYU professor, with several academics, artists, teachers, retail workers, and accountants discussed ways to take advantage of the emotion of the Occupy Movement to trigger a debt resistance movement within it. They decided their best chance would be to organize student debtors. There are millions of them who collectively owe nearly $1 trillion. (Spies)

Even some top economists seem to support the concept of punishing the creditors and relieving the debtors, basically blaming the people who loan money more than those who borrow it. When Iceland did exactly that in response to its financial crisis, Nobel Prize winner Joeseph Stilitz said he thought Iceland did the right thing by letting the banks fail because he did not think future generations should suffer from current failures in the financial system. (Bowers)

I wonder how Stilitz believes future generations will not feel the impact of Iceland's collapse when thousands lost all of their savings and thousands more are still underwater on their mortgages? I have read a lot about the Iceland situation. It was so bad that there was and still is no easy way out. Everyone has suffered and a lot of suffering remains.

A National Borrowing Moratorium

What if everyone just stopped borrowing for a few months? It may surprise people to learn this would be an even bigger economic disaster. Remember, our economic growth is based on borrowing and spending. We stop borrowing, the balloon deflates and the economy with it.

If we borrow too much, the debt burden crushes us. If we stop borrowing, deflation crushes us. A real Catch 22 isn't it? Perhaps the biggest Catch 22 in human history considering the U.S. economy is the largest in history.

Too Big to Bail

What happens if a major rupture in our debt balloon does occur? No one can bail us out. The $60 trillion debt of the US economy is equal to about 85% of the total GDP of the world; currently about $71 trillion. So the U.S. economic collapse would not be like Greece, or Italy, or Spain. Odds are it would be more like Iceland which saw its GDP decline by 40% in 24 months. Five years after Iceland's economy hit its peak GDP of $20 billion, it is still 33% below its peak and actually dropped 2012 – 2013.

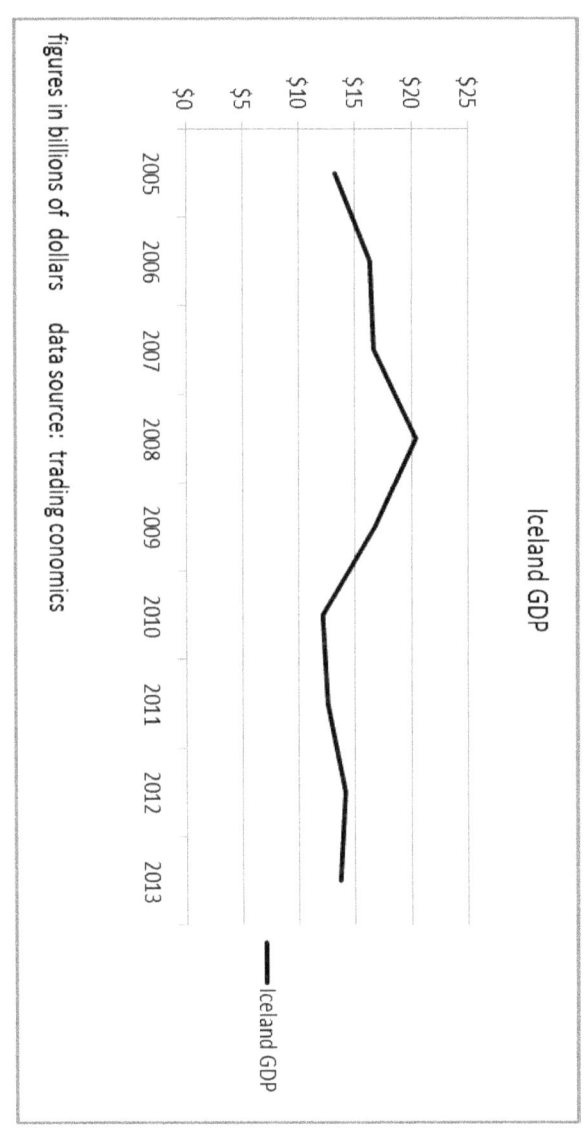

Graph 15

Iceland reacted to its crisis in exactly the opposite way of the U.S. Iceland let its banks fail rather than bail them out. Some economists hailed this move as "the right thing to do"; however this move did cause great pain to honest investors and savers in those banks who collectively lost millions. So the question I would ask is "right thing to do for whom?" There is no good answer as everyone suffered.

It is notable that this collapse resulted in large scale social unrest triggering a sort of bloodless revolution that put bankers and politicians in jail while appointing a citizen's government. **M.J. Bryant, a professor at the Ivey Business School in Canada who has written case studies on Iceland uses the Richter scale to compare the U.S. 2008 crisis to Iceland's giving the U.S. a 3 and Iceland a 9.** (Popper)

For more info on Iceland, see Appendix C

What do the experts say?

Expert opinions on where our economy is headed range from doomsday to euphoria, even among Nobel Prize winning economists. The euphoric ones tend to be Keynesians, as is Janet Yellen, the new Chairperson of the Federal Reserve. If we look back in history a bit, to the 1925 – 1940 period, we also find euphoric economists, including John Maynard Keynes himself making some bold statements about the future. Let's see how their economic predictions worked out for the country.

"I cannot help but raise a dissenting voice to statements that we are living in a fool's paradise, and that prosperity in this country must necessarily diminish and recede in the near future." E. H. H. Simmons, President, New York Stock Exchange, January 12, 1928.

"Stock prices have reached what looks like a

permanently high plateau. I do not feel there will be soon if ever a 50 or 60 point break from present levels, such as (bears) have predicted. I expect to see the stock market a good deal higher within a few months." Irving Fisher, Ph.D. in economics, Oct. 17, 1929, a few days before the 1929 market crash.

"We will not have any more crashes in our time." John Maynard Keynes, 1937. (The stock market lost 50% of its value in the next year and Keynes' personal investments were nearly wiped out.)

Are today's economists smarter than they were? I think today's economists have better tools and far more data to work with, but do not see much evidence it has made them any better at forecasting the economy.

A Gathering of Nobel Prize Winning Economists

73 economists have been awarded The Nobel Prize since 1969. (See appendix A for a list of them.)

As I was reading a little about each one's accomplishments, it dawned on me that about the only thing all 73 Nobel Prize winners agree on is that 72 of them are wrong about something. Anyone who has had an interest in economics, finance or the stock market has heard the jokes forever; "How do you start a fight? Ask two economists to agree on something." "How do you forecast the stock market? 1. Roll a pair of dice 2. Ask an economist to roll a pair of dice for you." Etc. etc. etc. But are the jokes fair?
It turns out the economists have good reason to doubt each other as studies have shown economists and finance professionals in general have a poor record when it comes to making any kind of forecast or prediction about the economy.

Perhaps the most extensive study was conducted by Philip Tetlock. He compared over 82,000 forecasts by over 300 experts in finance and the economy to what actually happened. He found using a dart board would have been about as accurate as most of them. Even more surprising, he found the most famous of the group were in the lowest performers in terms of accuracy. But why are they the most popular if their results are so poor? In general, because they are the best communicators and most willing to step up on the public stage to use their persuasiveness to convince others they are right. And of course, once they make their prediction so public, they dare not back away from it. (Schurenberg)

It would be silly and unfair to question the intelligence of these people who have dedicated their lives to studying and attempting to understand how the economy works. It is fair to question how these very intelligent, dedicated professionals can study and analyze the same economic data with such intensity then come up with different, sometimes exactly the opposite conclusions. The Nobel Prize winners for economics in 2013 are the most recent and perhaps best examples of this.

Robert J. Shiller, famous for the "Shiller Index" and even more famous for coining the term "housing bubble" in 2005, predicted housing prices would fall by 40% in the not too distant future. It took until 2008 to hit but by 2009 his prediction was looking pretty accurate. Still, that was not enough to earn him any respect from his equally well known opponents. Some said he was just lucky. One in particular, the creator of Rational Market Theory Eugene F. Fama, was a bit more critical. According the Mr. Fama there are no such things as bubbles in the economy therefore the use of the term bubble has no meaning.

These two exceptionally intelligent gentlemen, Robert J Shiller and Eugene F Fama, whom everyone knows are on opposite sides of a critical topic in financial planning, are never-the-less the co-winners of the 2013 Nobel Prize in Economics. (Appelbaum)

Conclusion: We can find a Nobel Prize winning economist to support pretty much whatever we already believe. But why is this? The explanation I have read that makes the most sense to me concerns the basic approach to the study of macro-economics. Most economists approach it as a rational, scientific study of complex data accumulated from trillions of financial transactions. The idea is that there is some magic formula that will predict how the economy will move next based on how it has moved in the past. This assumes the economy is defined by the financial transactions. But is it?

A different view is that the economy is defined by millions, even billions of human beings making emotional, often irrational decisions about what they will buy, sell or borrow. And as far as I have been able to determine, there is no rational scientific method that can predict irrational human behavior of an individual or a mass of people. One notable economist who is brave enough to openly express this idea is Alan Greenspan; Chairman of the Federal Reserve of the United States from 1987 to 2006.

During an interview on The Daily Show with Jon Stewart September 19, 2007, Greenspan said "I was telling my colleagues the other day… I'd been dealing with these big mathematical models for forecasting the economy, and I'm looking at what's going on the last few weeks and I say, "Y'know, if I could figure out a way to determine whether or not people are more fearful, or changing to euphoric… I don't need any of this other stuff. I could forecast the economy better than any way I know. The trouble is, we can't figure that out. I've been in the forecasting business for 50 years, and I'm no better than I ever was, and nobody else is either."

Maybe our Nobel Prize economists could do a better job of forecasting if they had a Ph.D. in Psychology rather than economics.

When Will It Burst?

We can predict with 100% accuracy that a balloon will burst if we continue to fill it with air. We cannot predict exactly where the rupture in the surface will begin or under how much pressure. It is not technically feasible to analyze every one of the trillions of molecular bonds on the surface to determine which one is slightly weaker than the others and under what exact pressure the first bond will fail.

The problem with the US economy is exactly the same. It is far too complex to collect all the data necessary fast enough and analyze it in relation to all the other data to determine which segment of the economy is slightly weaker than the others at any given time or under what debt load that segment will fail. But we can predict with 100% accuracy that as long as we keep pumping debt into the economy, it will eventually collapse. It does not mean the end of the world, but it does mean a big adjustment to life styles.

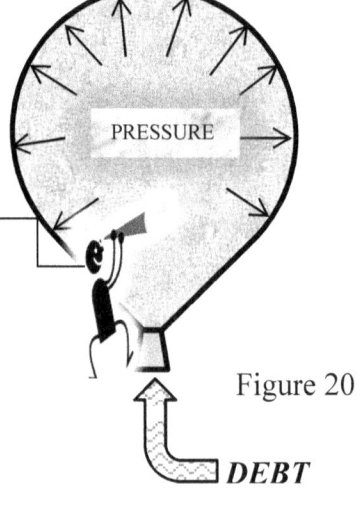

I found it! The electromagnetic force at energy level three of this carbon atom is definitely slightly less than the third energy level of the other trillion atoms, maybe.

PRESSURE

Figure 20

DEBT

I am quite certain the end of the debt based economic system will not be triggered by a specific GDP to debt ratio, or hitting a certain level of foreclosures, or passing a benchmark in credit card defaults. These data points may correlate to a change but they will not cause it because people on the street do not make their financial decisions based on any of these things. Most people on the street do not know these things exist much less monitor them. People make their decisions on what to buy, when to buy it and how much if any to borrow to buy it based on their personal situation, advice from people they trust and a general cultural attitude to some extent.

It is a good bet the government will not lead in trying to fundamentally change directions economically. It has too must vested in the one we have now, both politically and financially, in that it has made so many of the top party supporters on all sides so much money.

Right now I would put my money on the generation that has been so heavily involved in driving every cultural shift for the last fifty years, my generation, the Baby Boomers. But this time it will not be because they are looking forward. It will be because they are looking back with regrets and leading by bad example.

The oldest of the Boomers are turning 68 this year. But the big news is not how many are retiring. It is how many cannot afford to. The youngest Boomers are turning 50 this year. They should be ramping up their retirement savings, but they cannot. Many are supporting parents with healthcare problems. Many others are supporting unemployed or underemployed adult children. And far too many find themselves pinched between those two generations. So many Boomers have borrowed and spent their retirement that millions of them now plan on working into their seventies if they can, or retiring with no savings, still paying for mortgages, student loans they co-signed for and maxed out credit cards.

As this happens, the children and grandchildren of Boomers are learning through personal experience what living beyond your means on debt does to your life in the end. And the Boomers are starting to tell them "Don't be like me". I believe the only reason our debt based economy has worked as long as it has is because the Boomers bought into it lock, stock and barrel. What I think will end the debt based economy is the refusal of enough people to buy in to it on the advice of the Boomers.

There are some early signs the financial crisis of 2008 may have started this cultural shift already. While the marketing firms are still promoting the glamor of zero interest balance transfers, we are seeing a significant increase in media reporting and investigation of the evils of debt.

CNBC ran a special series called *Til Debt Do You Part* (Vaz-Oxlade)

The New York Times ran a whole series of articles called *The Debt Trap (The Debt Trap)*

Talk show hosts on financial advice programs, like Suze Orman, spend a large amount of time discussing the evils of debt and how to manage them. (Orman)

Are they having an impact on the big picture yet? There is not much evidence they are. I believe that is because these programs and these traditional media outlets in general appeal more to the generation in trouble, the Boomers, than to the generations that need to learn not to get in debt in the first place. I know many high school and college kids who barely know the traditional media outlets exist. When we see The Daily Show with Jon Stewart doing satires of the debt stories appearing on the mainstream media outlets, we will know something serious is happening out there.

Glad I Am Debt Free!

Personal debt councilors, financial planners, etc. will certainly agree people who are debt free are in a better position than people who are not. Unfortunately, everyone ends up sharing the burden of the total debt of our economy in the end no matter what their personal situation is. Who paid for the bailouts in 2008, 2009? Who saw their asset values decline? (Houses, stock, etc.) Who lost their jobs? Did anyone ask them if they were in debt or not first? Nope. Don't care. And if it is as bad as Iceland, which let its banks fail, the debt free savers will still lose all of their savings.

An equal share of the current $59 trillion debt for each and every man, woman and child in the United States right now would be $186,092.71. Of course, not everyone will end up paying the same price. That is life as we know it.

Is There a Way Out?

I don't know. If all the great economic minds cannot agree on what we can do about it, how should I know? I did not write this book as a set up to sell you gold, tell you to buy food insurance, suggest building a survival bunker, take a survival course or attend a paramilitary training camp to prepare to defend yourself.

But there is one thing I am sure of; when the balloon bursts, there will be a mad, desperate witch hunt for somebody holding a pin. Right in front of the lynch mob, screaming for justice, carrying torches and pitch forks, will be the very people responsible for filling the balloon full of hot air in the first place, our political leaders. The person, party and/or policy in place at the moment the economy takes a dive will end up taking a dive with it.

I wrote this book so everyone who reads it will hopefully understand whatever happens with our economy is the result of 50 years of intentional fiscal policy by people who knew exactly what they were doing. But with the way our political system works, these people also knew they would get credit for short term benefits and not be held responsible for anything bad that happened long term.

Americans in general are financially illiterate and have the attention span of a goldfish. As long as everything holds together until the current elected official or appointed bureaucrat finishes his or her term, he or she will be forgotten in the blink of an eye. As for the people in charge who put us on this path in the 1960s, they are not only forgotten, they are no longer of this Earth.

My Conclusions

As I have researched and read through the facts and conclusions reached by others mentioned in this book, and many more not mentioned in this book, I have developed my own conclusions. I am not telling, or even asking you to agree with them. I would prefer you review the facts for yourself and draw your own conclusions.

While studying some of the various economies through history, a pattern seemed to emerge. The economies, no matter what they were based on or how they were created, had a life cycle.

Birth or creation as you prefer
They evolved to fit a need to provide a medium of exchange for trading goods and services.

Rapid growth
They grew as they became successful at filling that need and enabling more economic activity.

Maturity
The infrastructure of the economy reached its capacity to support economic activity.

Decline
The infrastructure begins to break down under the pressure
to expand the economy further.

Disease and death
The infrastructure supporting the economy weakens and
collapses.

The length and size of each segment of the cycle
appears to be unique to each economic situation and system,
but they all eventually died.

The commodity based economic system established
by Bretton-Woods served the needs of the United States
until fiscal and policy decisions made in the 1960s made it
unworkable. So it was dropped in 1971 in favor of our
current debt based economic system. It met the immediate
need of allowing the U.S. government to print enough
money to pay its bills. It met longer term goals of growing
the economy by increasing the number of ways, the
amounts, and the ease of spending more by borrowing more.
However, after 37 years of increasing debt, 2008
demonstrated the risk and limits of using debt to grow an
economy.

One economic system that lasted centuries evolved
in the Roman Empire. It was largely based on confiscation
of wealth. Rome sent its armies out to conquer new lands.
They confiscated anything with value and sent it back to
Rome, including food and slaves to provide cheap labor. It
worked well as long as there were new lands to conquer.
But by the second century, when Rome had expanded
across all of Europe, there was not much left to confiscate,
including new slaves, which put great pressure on the
Roman economy. By the fifth century, Vandals cut Rome's
ability to import wealth further by capturing North Africa
and putting pirate ships across the Mediterranean. Many

historians consider the impact of this economic pressure as a factor in the fall of the Roman Empire. (Andrews)

Keep in mind the fall of Rome and its economy took centuries. The modern world we live in operates on a slightly faster timetable.

Just as Rome ran out of new territories to conquer to support its economy, creditors in the United States are running out of new markets to exploit to keep our debt based economy growing. And the existing markets are near being maxed out, if not there already.

After studying the progression of debt use in the United States, I believe our economic system is in decline, perhaps even the early stage of disease.

1. The rate of growth of our GDP has been declining.

2. The amount of debt it takes to generate a given amount of GDP has increased steadily and dramatically.

3. There are not any new debt markets to exploit.
   a. We have expanded debt by getting more people to borrow more for the last 50 years with credit cards, home equity loans, longer car loans, larger student loans, etc.
   b. Savings, the primary source for funds to loan, have dramatically decreased
   c. The federal government's ability to print money to give to the banks to loan is limited by inflation potential
   d. Creditors are becoming less willing to lend money to higher risk borrowers

4. The wealth gap between the richest and everyone else is increasing dramatically

5. The United States government and financial leaders are not discussing the issue of total debt expansion. Some ignore it. Others say outright "It is not our concern."

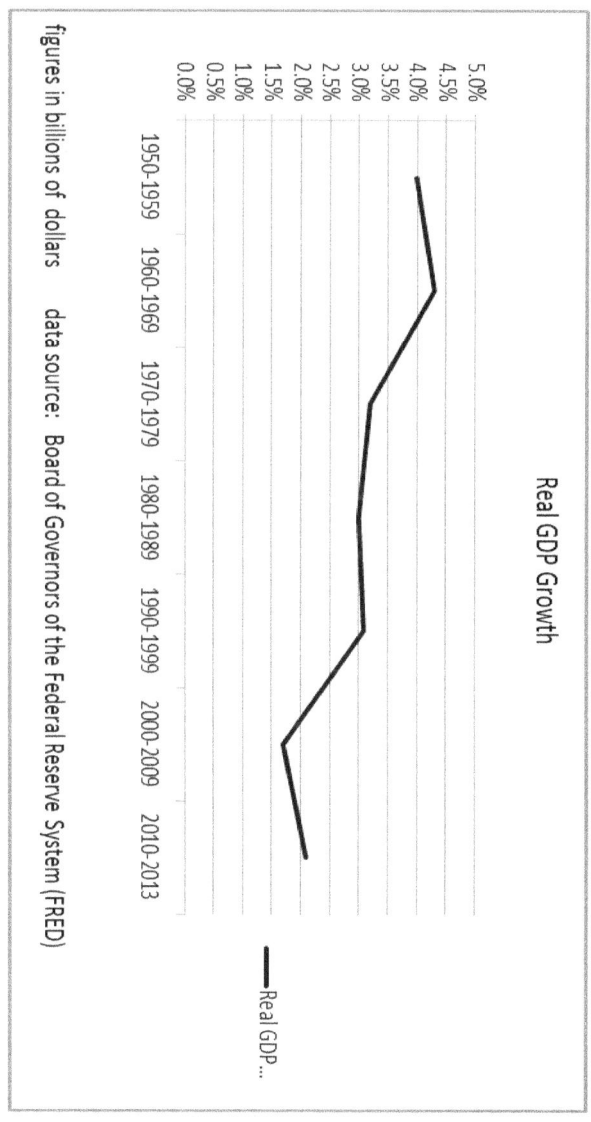

Graph 16

So where does that leave us?

- The basis for our current economic system will eventually fail
- The death of one system is the birth of a new system
- It will not be the end of the world
- I will not be the end of civilization
- Humans will not become extinct
- Culture, technology and agriculture will not disappear
- There will be great suffering by a great number of people
- It will impact the availability, distribution and use of scarce resources
- The competition for the scarce resources may lead to wars.

NOTE; Studies by the U.N. and others predict shortages of water in particular have already caused armed conflicts and will cause more with or without an economic collapse. But there is no question an economic collapse would make conflicts more likely and potentially more severe.

Former U.S. Secretary of State Hillary Clinton and the InterAction Council, an association of 37 former heads of state and government declared the growing shortage of water to be an urgent security issue, far more so than any potential shortage of oil. It is estimated 1.2 – 1.7 billion people already face shortages and supplies are drying up fast. (Leahy)

What Can We Do?

The first step to solving a problem, no matter how large, is admitting we have one. Our political, financial, and business leaders have yet to agree on this much less try to do anything about it.

The second step is to clearly understand and define the problem. This would require a non-partisan, unbiased, intense effort by some very intelligent people without influence or interference by political agendas of major political parties. (Good luck with that happening today.)

Unless we start electing candidates who do not owe their political careers and opportunities to profit after them, to the agenda of a major political party, I do not think we will see any change in our current direction economically or politically, no matter which party has control. We will continue to 'borrow blindly into oblivion'. Remember, it has made no difference which party had control of our government over the last fifty years in getting us to where we are now.

In other words, voters have the power to ignore the political propaganda machines, ignore the candidates backed by big money, and scare the daylights out of Washington D.C. by sending it a wave of the least known, least connected candidates in the elections who have no reason to listen to the party bosses. Or we can keep voting as we have the last fifty years and get the same results, or worse.

The odds of this shift in voting patterns occurring are not favorable, but it is statistically possible. There are over 70 million members of the Baby Boomers out there between 50 and 68 years old. No candidate for President has ever picked up 70 million votes. If the generation that led a social revolution in the 1960s came together with a singular purpose in mind, they could do it again. It probably sounds crazy, but I have a feeling deep in the pit of my stomach that the Boomers are not about to fade quietly into the sunset.

Final Reflection

As I was going through all this material for the 100th time, checking grammar, citations, spelling and such, I could not shake the feeling I was missing something; something simple yet illusive.

I started this project a year ago, the first time I saw a TCDMO chart. My first impression was "How in the world did we let this happen?" Then I realized it really is simple. All of the thousands of pages written about the Great Recession can be summed up in a single sentence;

"People borrowed too much money."

Everything that happened in 2008 was the result of this one simple, undisputed fact. So what were the thousands of pages of analysis all about? Other questions like who borrowed too much money? Who do we blame for people borrowing too much money? Why did people borrow too much money?

Why indeed. Because we are people: that is why.

Why do overweight people continue to over eat?

Why do people who smoke keep smoking even after they get sick?

Why do people who gamble keep gambling when they have nothing left to gamble with?

Why do people keep getting married when half end up divorced?

Why do writers keep writing when no one buys their books?

People make emotional, irrational, compulsive decisions on a regular basis. When we want something and someone tells us we can have it, we take it, even when we know it will be bad for us; especially if it is money.

This is why I believe no economist will ever be able to come up with a scientific model that consistently and accurately forecasts the economy. Our economy is made up of irrational, emotional, unpredictable human beings who will do what they want no matter what the models say they should do; especially us Boomers.

And with that, good night.

Appendix A: List of Nobel Prize Economists

1969	Ragnar Frisch	Norway
	Jan Tinbergen	Netherlands
1970	Paul A. Samuelson	United States
1971	Simon Kuznets	United States
1972	Kenneth J. Arrow	United States
	John R. Hicks	Great Britain
1973	Wassily Leontief	United States
1974	Gunnar Myrdal	Sweden
	Friedrich A. von Hayek	Austria
1975	Tjalling Koopmans	Netherlands - United States
	Leonid Kantorovich	Soviet Union
1976	Milton Friedman	United States
1977	Bertil Ohlin	Sweden
	James E. Meade	Great Britain
1978	Herbert A. Simon	United States
1979	Theodore W. Schultz	United States
	Sir Arthur Lewis	Great Britain
1980	Lawrence R. Klein	United States
1981	James Tobin	United States
1982	George J. Stigler	United States
1983	Gerard Debreu	France - United States
1984	Richard Stone	Great Britain
1985	Franco Modigliani	Italy - United States

1986	James M. Buchanan	United States
1987	Robert M. Solow	United States
1988	Maurice Allais	France
1989	Trygve Haavelmo	Norway
1990	Harry M. Markowitz William F. Sharpe Merton H. Miller	United States United States United States
1991	Ronald H. Coase	Great Britain - United States
1992	Gary S. Becker	United States
1993	Robert W. Fogel Douglass C. North	United States United States
1994	John C. Harsanyi John F. Nash Reinhard Selten	United States United States Germany
1995	Robert E. Lucas, Jr.	United States
1996	James A. Mirrlees William Vickrey	Great Britain Canada - United States
1997	Robert C. Merton Myron S. Scholes	United States Canada - United States
1998	Amartya Sen	India
1999	Robert A. Mundell	Canada
2000	James J. Heckman Daniel L. McFadden	United States United States
2001	George A. Akerlof A. Michael Spence	United States United States

	Joseph E. Stiglitz	United States
2002	Daniel Kahneman	United States - Israel
	Vernon L. Smith	United States
2003	Robert F. Engle III	United States
	Clive W.J. Granger	United Kingdom
2004	Finn E. Kydland	Norway
	Edward C. Prescott	United States
2005	Robert J. Aumann	Israel - United States
	Thomas C. Schelling	United States
2006	Edmund S. Phelps	United States
2007	Leonid Hurwicz	United States
	Eric S. Maskin	United States
	Roger B. Myerson	United States
2008	Paul Krugman	United States
2009	Elinor Ostrom	United States
	Oliver E. Williamson	United States
2010	Peter A. Diamond	United States
	Dale T. Mortensen	United States
	Christopher A. Pissarides	Cyprus
2011	Thomas J. Sargent	United States
	Christopher A. Sims	United States
2013	**Eugene F. Fama**	United States
	Lars Peter Hansen	United States
	Robert J. Shiller	United States

Appendix B TCDMO and GDP Data by Year

FRED Graph Observations

Federal Reserve Bank

Year	TCMDO	GDP
1949-01-01	#N/A	271.0
1950-01-01	425.38	320.3
1951-01-01	449.34	356.6
1952-01-01	484.70	381.2
1953-01-01	516.70	386.5
1954-01-01	541.81	400.3
1955-01-01	582.03	437.8
1956-01-01	611.49	461.3
1957-01-01	642.70	475.7
1958-01-01	681.55	500.4
1959-01-01	738.75	529.3
1960-01-01	780.25	541.1
1961-01-01	828.55	581.6
1962-01-01	888.18	613.1
1963-01-01	954.18	654.8
1964-01-01	1028.51	698.4
1965-01-01	1106.85	773.1
1966-01-01	1187.26	834.9
1967-01-01	1267.95	883.2
1968-01-01	1372.91	970.1
1969-01-01	1490.61	1040.7
1970-01-01	1599.56	1091.5
1971-01-01	1749.54	1193.6
1972-01-01	1933.55	1332.0
1973-01-01	2170.75	1479.1
1974-01-01	2407.98	1603.0
1975-01-01	2616.33	1765.9
1976-01-01	2904.06	1938.4
1977-01-01	3291.72	2168.7

1978-01-01	3776.28	2482.2
1979-01-01	4273.69	2730.7
1980-01-01	4722.38	2993.5
1981-01-01	5255.05	3283.5
1982-01-01	5766.80	3407.8
1983-01-01	6462.89	3796.1
1984-01-01	7422.53	4147.6
1985-01-01	8719.65	4453.1
1986-01-01	9909.59	4669.4
1987-01-01	10928.07	5022.7
1988-01-01	11957.78	5412.7
1989-01-01	12913.41	5763.4
1990-01-01	13827.68	6023.3
1991-01-01	14481.20	6279.3
1992-01-01	15265.24	6697.5
1993-01-01	16339.09	7032.8
1994-01-01	17420.60	7476.6
1995-01-01	18649.12	7799.5
1996-01-01	19969.11	8287.0
1997-01-01	21386.13	8788.3
1998-01-01	23468.99	9325.6
1999-01-01	25524.43	9932.3
2000-01-01	27254.73	10475.3
2001-01-01	29433.29	10702.7
2002-01-01	31940.09	11105.7
2003-01-01	34745.38	11818.5
2004-01-01	38710.44	12563.8
2005-01-01	42194.43	13383.3
2006-01-01	46347.44	14068.4
2007-01-01	51130.99	14690.0
2008-01-01	53581.83	14546.7
2009-01-01	53489.48	14564.1
2010-01-01	53842.79	15231.7
2011-01-01	54983.29	15818.7
2012-01-01	56981.50	16420.3
2013-01-01	58991.39	17089.6

Appendix C Suggested Reading Material

On the danger of private debt growth

High debt squeezes headroom for growth, economists warn

This article presents the views of Australian economics professor Steve Keen on the close correlation between growth of private debt and recessions. (Deboonme)

Recent research indicates that rising private-debt levels also endanger growth.

A report and analysis of a paper by Moritz Schularick, now at the University of Bonn, and Alan Taylor, at the University of Virginia, about the link between private debt growth and financial crisis from 1870 to 2008 (Economist, staff)

Looking Back To 1870, An Economist Found A Link Between Private Debt And Recessions

Another, more detailed look at Alan Taylor's study and how it relates to our current economic situation. (Economist)

Private debt is the millstone that holds back enterprise – and a better future

An Irish article examining the impact of private debt on economic growth noting that the biggest concern is debt that cannot and will not be paid back.(Maguire)

On the dangers of total debt growth

Reaching Debt Limits: With or without China's problems, we have a problem

An article looking at a study of eight centuries of financial crisis and how total debt played a role while noting all the emphasis on China's economic situation is detracting from the real problems in the U.S.

Usury in the USA

This is an interesting look at the state of the U.S. Economy from an Asian perspective, Hong Kong in particular, by a UCLA educated Ph.D. in Economics. (Krichene)

On the dangers of debt in retirement

The Real Debt Crisis We Aren't Talking About

This article takes a hard look at the financial situation of the seniors, Baby Boomers in particular, and how their debt will impact the economy for the next 20-30 years. (Foroohar)

The Frightening Facts About America's Retirement Crisis

 Another article looking at the financial difficulties of seniors in America with many statistics on employment, debt, savings, etc. (Alix)

On the dangers of margin debt

NYSE Margin Debt Hits Record $451 Billion; Watch Out If Rate Drops

An article detailing the rise of margin debt and what it could mean to the stock market. (Fisher)

On the dangers of student loan debt

Student Loans Hit Record $1.08 Trillion; Delinquent Student Debt Rises To All Time High

A detailed article on the rise of student loan debt, the impact of non-payments, and the future impacts as totals grow. (Durden)

On the dangers of consumer debt

Rising consumer debt also linked to lackluster retail results

An article examining the negative impact of consumer debt on growth in consumer retail sales, disputing that bad weather was the primary cause of slow winter sales. (Souza)

On the end of the gold standard

Black Gold – The End of Bretton-Woods and the Oil Price Shocks of the 1970s

This is a very detailed and interesting analysis of how the end of the Bretton-Woods Agreement resulted in the Oil Shock of the mid 1970s and what it did to the U.S. economy. (Hammes)

August 15, 1971: A Date Which Has Lived In Infamy

This article takes a large view on how ending the Bretton-Woods Agreement put us in a whole new economic era which we have little understanding of. (Domitrovic)

The Nixon Shock Heard 'Round the World

An article from the Wall Street Journal detailing the impact of going off the gold standard highlighting the fact that the purchasing value of a dollar has dropped to 18 cents compared to what is was on August 14, 1971. (Lehman)

Nixon and the End of the Bretton Woods System, 1971–1973

This is a very objective look at the details of how the Bretton-Woods Agreement came to an end and what happened afterward by the Department of State Office of the Historian

The Iceland economic crisis

Total Banking Collapse, A Timeline

A detailed timeline of the banking collapse in Iceland from the early '90s and to the present day. It accompanies the article The Collapse And Beyond. (Benjamin)

Iceland rises from the ashes of banking collapse

A look at the Iceland situation from a UK viewpoint that also finds economists delight at letting banks fail pitted against the realities of what that has done to the people in Iceland and the large number of UK residents who innocently invested their savings in the failed banks.(Bowers)

The Collapse And Beyond

A detailed study of what various economists think about the economic collapse in Iceland and the following attempt at recovery as compared to what the people in Iceland actually feel and are enduring, which is quit different in many ways, with the external economists far more positve about it in general than the people who are living with it. (Davíðsdóttir)

Works Cited

Alix, Amanda. "The Frightening Facts About America's
Retirement Crisis." *The Frightening Facts About
America's Retirement Crisis*. The Motley Fool, 23
Mar. 2014. Web. 04 May 2014.

Andrews, Evan. "8 Reasons Why Rome Fell." *History.com*.
A&E Television Networks, 14 Jan. 2014. Web. 03
May 2014.

Appelbaum, Binyamin. "Economists Clash on Theory, but
Will Still Share the Nobel." *The New York Times*.
The New York Times, 14 Oct. 2013. Web. 04 May
2014.

Barnet, Juan. "Automotive Financing and the Pursuit
of Happiness." *Autobytel*. Autobytel, Inc., 27 June
2013. Web. 26 Apr. 2014.

Benjamin, Tomas G. "The Reykjavík Grapevine." *The
Reykjavik Grapevine Features / Total Banking
Collapse, A Timeline*.
Http://www.grapevine.is/Features/ReadArticle/Tota
l-Banking-Collapse-A-Timeline, 10 Sept. 2013.
Web. 29 Apr. 2014.

Bowers, Simon. "Iceland Rises from the Ashes of
Banking Collapse." *The Guardian*. Guardian News
and Media, 07 Oct. 2013. Web. 29 Apr. 2014.

Brooks, Rodney. "Retirement Living: Debt Holds
Many Boomers Back." *USA Today*. Gannett, 21 Oct.
2013. Web. 04 May 2014.

Bryan, Dan. "Give Me Liberty or Give Me Debt – A
History of Credit Cards." *American History USA
RSS*. American History USA, 1 July 2012. Web. 03
May 2014.

Clinch, Matt. "Warning Signs? Margin Debt Soars
Again." *CNBC.com*. CNBC, 31 Mar. 2014. Web. 04
May 2014.

Cox, Jeff. "Corporate Debt Fever Surges to New
Record." *CNBC.com*. CNBC, 10 Mar. 2014. Web.
04 May 2014.

Davíðsdóttir, Sigrún. "The Reykjavík Grapevine." *The
Reykjavik Grapevine*. The Reykjavík Grapevine, 10
Apr. 213. Web. 29 Apr. 2014.

Deboonme, Achara. "High Debt Squeezes Headroom
for Growth, Economists Warn." *The Nation*. Nation
Multimedia, 2 Dec. 2013. Web. 04 May 2014.

Domitrovic, Brian. "August 15, 1971: A Date Which
Has Lived In Infamy." *Forbes*. Forbes Magazine,
14 Aug. 2011. Web. 29 Apr. 2014.

Durden, Tyler. "Student Loans Hit Record $1.08
Trillion; Delinquent Student Debt Rises To All
Time High." *Zero Hedge*., 18 Feb. 014. Web. 29
Apr. 2014.

Economist, Staff. "Breaking the Threshold." *The
Economist*. The Economist Newspaper, 01 Mar.
2014. Web. 04 May 2014.

Economist, The. "Looking Back To 1870, An
    Economist Found A Link Between Private Debt
    And Recessions." *Business Insider*. Business Insider,
    Inc, 04 Sept. 2012. Web. 26 Apr. 2014.

Fisher, Daniel. "NYSE Margin Debt Hits Record $451
    Billion; Watch Out If Rate Drops." *Forbes*. Forbes
    Magazine, 03 Mar. 2014. Web. 29 Apr. 2014.

Foroohar, Rana. "The Real Debt Crisis We Aren't
    Talking About." *Time*. Time, 14 Mar. 2014. Web.
    04 May 2014.

Hammes, David, and Douglas Wills. *Black Gold – The
    End of Bretton-Woods and the Oil Price Shocks of
    the 1970s*. University of Washington, Spring 2005.
    Web. 28 Apr. 2014.

Historian, Office Of. "Nixon and the End of the Bretton
    Woods System." *Nixon and the End of the Bretton
    Woods System, 1971–1973 - 1969–1976 -
    Milestones - Office of the Historian*. United States
    Department of State, 21 Oct. 2013. Web. 28 Apr.
    2014.

Kolb, Charles. "August 15, 1971." *The Huffington Post*.
    TheHuffingtonPost.com, 19 Nov. 2013. Web. 03
    May 2014.

Krichene, Noureddine. "Asia Times Online :: Usury in
    the USA." *Asia Times Online :: Usury in the USA*.
    Asia Times Online, 14 Mar. 2014. Web. 04 May
    2014

Krugman, Paul. "Life Without Bubbles." *The New York
    Times*. The New York Times, 21 Dec. 2008. Web.
    26 Apr. 2014.

Leahy, Stephen. "Water Crisis Hitting Food, Energy –
　　And Everything Else - Inter Press Service." *Inter
　　Press Service*. Inter Press Service, 22 Mar. 2013.
　　Web. 04 May 2014.

Lehman, Lewis E. "The Nixon Shock Heard 'Round
　　the World." *The Wall Street Journal*. Dow Jones &
　　Company, 15 Aug. 2011. Web. 29 Apr. 2014.

Maguire, Ross. "Column: Private Debt Is the Millstone
　　That Holds Back Enterprise – and a Better Future."
　　TheJournalie. Journal Media Ltd., 26 Feb. 2014.
　　Web. 04 May 2014.

Michael, Geoffrey. "The Dangers Of Deflation."
　　Investopedia. Investopedia, 16 Mar. 2011. Web. 04
　　May 2014.

Miquelon, Cameron. "More Trade-Ins Pulled
　　Underwater As Negative Equity Level Rises." *The
　　Truth About Cars*. The Truth About Cars, 24 Apr.
　　2014. Web. 26 Apr. 2014.

Morgon, John. "A Ghost of the Housing Meltdown
　　Returns: HELOCs Are Baaack." *Moneynews*. News
　　Max Media, Inc, 10 Mar. 2014. Web. 26 Apr. 2014.

Orman, Suzie. "Managing Debt." *Managing Debt*.
　　Suze Orman Media, Inc., 1 June 2014. Web. 04
　　May 2014.

Popper, Nathaniel. "After Crisis, Iceland Holds a Tight
　　Grip on Its Banks." *DealBook After Crisis Iceland
　　Holds a Tight Grip on Its Banks Comments*. New
　　York Times, 15 Jan. 2014. Web. 04 May 2014.

Prevost, Lisa. "Carrying Debt After Retirement." *The New York Times*. The New York Times, 28 Sept. 2013. Web. 04 May 2014.

Richter, Wolf. "Stocks On Speed: Leverage Spikes, As Does Risk Of Crash (Look At That Insane Chart!)." *InvestmentWatch RSS*. InestmentWatch, 14 Mar. 014. Web. 04 May 2014.

Schurenberg, Eric. "Why the Experts Missed the Crash." *CNNMoney*. Cable News Network, 18 Feb. 2009. Web. 04 May 2014.

Scoffield, Heather. "'There Will Be Blood'" *The Globe and Mail*. The Globe and Mai, Incl, 24 Feb. 2009. Web. 26 Apr. 2014.

Souza, Kim. "Rising Consumer Debt Also Linked to Lackluster Retail Results." *Business, Political, and Cultural News in Fort Smith and Northwest Arkansas*. The City Wire Media, 06 Mar. 2014. Web. 29 Apr. 2014.

Spies, Mike. "Student Debt Will Devour Us All. Here's a Solution --." *Vocativ*. Vocativ, 21 Mar. 2014. Web. 04 May 2014.

Story, Louise. "Home Equity Frenzy Was a Bank Ad Come True." *The New York Times*. The New York Times, 14 Aug. 2008. Web. 03 May 2014.

"The Debt Trap." *New York Times* 1 Jan. 2009, Business News sec.: n. pag. - *Series*. New York Times, 1 Jan. 2009. Web. 04 May 2014.

Tverberg, Gail. "Reaching Debt Limits: With or without China's Problems, We Have a Problem." *Our Finite World*. Our Finite World, 11 Mar. 2014. Web. 04 May 2014.

Vaz-Oxlade, Gail. "Til Debt Do Us Part." *Til Debt Do Us Part*. CNBC. New York, New York, *CNBC.com*. Web. 04 May 2014.

Quarterly Updates

Q1 2014 - U.S. Total Debt Balloons as GDP Stalls

The Federal Reserve Bank of St. Louis released the current data for the total debt in the United States Economy on June 5, 2014; All Sectors; Credit Market Instruments; Liability, Level (TCMDO). While people, companies and governments blamed bad weather for a dismal showing in economic activity, it appears they had little trouble finding their way to the banks to add on $471 billion in new debt.

Data from the Federal Reserve Bank of St. Louis

Quarter	Debt	GDP	Gap
(Figures in In billions of dollars)			
2013-01-01	$57,406	$16,535	$40,871
2013-04-01	$57,605	$16,661	$40,944
2013-07-01	$58,039	$16,912	$41,126
2013-10-01	$58,914	$17,089	$41,825
2014-01-01	$59,398	$16,918*	$42,480

*Second estimate lowered initial first quarter GDP estimate of $17,101 to $16,918

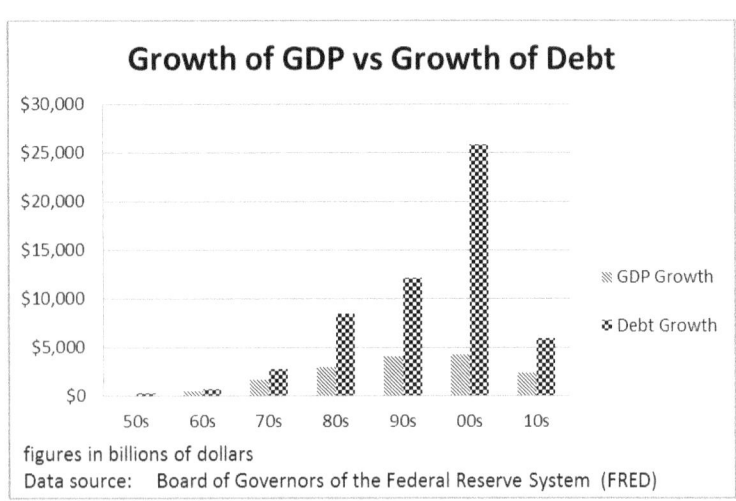

Reader Notes and Updates